No Place for a Prophet

C. Dexter Wise III

ISBN: 0-9621228-2-3. Cover Design by Foster and Foster, Inc. A *Wise Works, Inc.* Publication. PO Box 0771, Westerville, Ohio 43086. (614) 898-1997.

No Place for a Prophet!

Dedication

This book is dedicated to my beloved grandmother, Mrs. Sylvia Person. Word came to me of her death early in the morning of February 6, 1998 as I put the finishing touches on this work. She was without a doubt a sweet, smiling, sisterly, serving, interceding and singing saint who was deeply loved and will be greatly missed.

Thank you Grandmother!

Acknowledgments

With great gratitude and praise, I would like to acknowledge Almighty God for loving me, the Lord Jesus Christ for saving me, and the Holy Spirit for keeping me.

With great thanks and love, I would like to acknowledge my dear wife Shirley, who not only encouraged me to write this book, but who stood by me and with me through it all for more than twenty five years.

With great appreciation and pride, I would like to acknowledge our four children Sheri, Shonna, Ceylon and especially Sybil who helped with proof-reading and editing.

With great humility and joy, I would like to acknowledge everyone who has ever prayed for me; every hand which has ever helped me, and every enemy who has ever opposed me. Together, all of you have blessed my life and made me strong.

Dr. C. Dexter Wise III
Westerville, Ohio
April 1998

Traits of Traditional Churches

“Trapped”

Several years ago at the National Black Pastor’s Conference held in Chicago, I heard my role model, mentor and friend Bishop John R. Bryant preach a sermon. He entitled it: *“Trapped.”* He began what was to be another powerful, pentecostal experience with a litany of various people in our society who, in one way or another, often felt trapped.

He mentioned the hemmed in housewife, the hustling husband, the overworked hourly wage earner, the fenced in ghetto dweller, the mistreated American minorities and the discontented corporate executive. As I listened to the sermon, I could feel the pain of those about whom he spoke, but never once did I have a sense that he was talking about me.

I rejoiced when everyone else rejoiced. I said, “Amen” when everyone else said, “Amen.” I stood on my feet when everyone else stood on their feet. Nevertheless, I knew that he was not talking to me because I was not trapped.

In fact, at that time, I could honestly say that I had never *really* felt trapped. I was not born with a silver spoon in my mouth. I was acquainted with sorrow and had my share of grief, but never to the point that I saw *no* way out.

I had been raised in the ghetto, but I was not trapped. I applied to an Ivy League school with no money, but I was not trapped. I'd experienced trouble in my marriage, but I was not trapped. I had been arrested on mistaken identity, but I was not trapped. I had run short of money and had bill collectors calling my house so much that we developed a personal relationship, but still I was not trapped.

That is, not until several years later, during a prolonged and nasty church battle when I served as pastor of my second church. It was then that I knew what Bishop Bryant was talking about. The environment had become so polluted, the tension had become so great, the ministry had become so miserable that I couldn't breath. I couldn't think clearly. I couldn't find a reason for continuing. I couldn't see my way out. I couldn't imagine the pain ever letting up. I was trapped.

The irony of the whole thing is that I was trapped right in a large, respected, historic, and financially secure church.

Here I was, called to preach a liberating gospel from the pulpit of a place which had been designed to be a center of deliverance, and yet I was trapped. I made an excellent salary. I had great benefits. I drove a brand new Lincoln Town car. I lived in a big house in the suburbs. I was the envy of many of my peers and yet, I was trapped.

Hallowed walls were hollering at me. Bosom buddies were booing me. Seasoned saints were suing me. Preacher peers were critiquing me. The mass media was scrutinizing me. The devil was laughing at me. God was testing me. I was trapped.

Being trapped is never a matter of how much trouble you are in, but whether or not you can see your way out. That's why even though Joseph was in a pit, he was not trapped because he knew he had a dream to fulfill. That's why despite the fact that the Hebrew boys were facing the fiery furnace, they were not trapped because of their faith in a God who is able. That's why although Daniel was cast in the lion's den, he was not trapped because he believed in the power of prayer. That's why when Jesus was laid to rest in a borrowed tomb with a stone rolled in front of it, he was not trapped because he knew that he would rise again. In all of these seemingly difficult and desperate predicaments the people of faith in them did not feel trapped because each of them could somehow see their way out.

If anyone should have been able to see their way out, it should have been me. After all, I was the pastor. I was the moderator. I was the worship leader. I was the encourager. I was the speaker of the house. I was the CEO. Nevertheless, I felt trapped.

This present work has been written to retrace the steps of my journey over the past twenty some years as a pastor and to describe just how I became entangled in and liberated from the trappings of traditional churches.

It is not meant for revenge or to get back at anyone. God does that best. It is not meant to rewrite or revise a rough and rocky history. For, what is done is done. It is not even meant to recommend that others do as I have done. I would not wish my experience on another living soul.

Rather, the words which follow are a collection of reflections on how this preacher and other preachers can so easily become trapped in traditional churches; how they can avoid it; and how they can be delivered both in them and from them.

Therefore, if you are a preacher or pastor who knows what it means to be strangled by structure, intimidated by an institution, bound with by-laws, confined by constitutions, or bossed by boards, then this book is for you. If you are a preacher or pastor whose most precious proposals have never become programs, whose sanctified suggestions have never been given serious consideration or whose divinely inspired innovations have never been implemented, then this book is for you.

If you are the kind of preacher who may have all that a church can offer and still feel trapped, don't despair, this book is for you.

Stayed tuned for deliverance. For, if you hold out, deliverance surely will come. However, it will not come before we understand some of the troublesome traits of traditional churches, the common traps of typical preachers and the secrets to triumph for unconventional pastors.

History, But No Hallelujah

There are very few churches in America which could have boasted of more history than the church to which I was called in 1981. Chronologically, it was 113 years old. Traditionally, it was Black Baptist to the bone. Historically, it was a place which local, state and national events had for years regularly called home. Geographically, it was located in the center of what once was the heart of the Columbus, Ohio's Black community.

Politically, its parishioners were well connected and positioned in university, state and government jobs. Physically, it was at one time the largest Black church in the city. Socially, it was always at the forefront of social activism and change. Financially, it had a comfortable stash of cash in the bank. Denominationally, it was a charter member of the National Baptist Convention.

If its walls could talk they would tell of how the first Black elected to the Ohio State legislature, was one of that church's pastors when he ran and won. They would tell that the church supported a missionary in Africa; had a live radio broadcast in the 1930's and 1940's; hired a full time Director of Christian Education in the 1950's and opened the first church credit union in the city.

If its choir loft had a voice, it would sing of the concerts and soloists who were heard there. These included "Wings Over Jordan" and the church's own Senior Choir which was known to make people shout on an anthem!

If its pews could proclaim, they would list the various events such as the NAACP Convention and The National Baptist Congress which were once held in their laps. They would note that it was there that the Minister's Alliance of the city met every Monday; the Pastor's Conference met every first Tuesday; and the city-wide Seven Last Words observance was held every Good Friday.

If its pulpit could preach, it would recite the record of famous orators and celebrities who stood behind it. This would include, of course, its most well known pastors as well as occasional guests such as Rev. Jesse Jackson and President Jimmie Carter.

There is no question, this church was full of history. You could feel it when you walked in the door. However, with all of its history, there was something missing. By 1981, for sure, it had lost its hallelujah.

That is to say, most of what it had to look forward to was behind it.

Please don't get me wrong, I have nothing against history. In fact, many of our people are adrift on the sea of life simply because they do not know their history. However, if all you have to offer is history, then you have very little to hope for in the future.

My predecessor had retired after 35 years of outstanding ministry. The pulpit had been vacant for nearly five years. There was no significant number of young adults in the church and very few little children. To make matters worse, one of my buddies from Baltimore, had come to the city, a few years earlier and swept away many of the youth and young adults from that church and just about every other church in town.

The fact was that this church had the name and history of a great church, but it had not done anything particularly great recently. It was no longer the talk of the town. It had one of the largest sanctuaries in town, but it had far from the liveliest worships in town. It had a great host of choirs, but they sang: "Let mount Zion rejoice to death!" It used to be the *hot* spot in town, now without a pastor for five years, they had become the *not* spot in town.They were Cadillacs in a world of BMW's and they knew it.

No one ever told me in so many words, but it was everywhere to be seen and sensed in the not so casual comments and in the looks on people's faces. They knew they had once been at the top and they knew that they were no longer there.

Thus, what they wanted when they called a pastor was to get a man who could lead them back to the limelight, the spotlight, the forefront and the place of real prominence which they had enjoyed for so many years. So, with the hope that the good old days would return, this 113 year old church called me, a 27 year old preacher.

From day one, I knew what my assignment was and what the people expected. I was called there to help restore the hallelujah. Confident that it could be done, I immediately went about my work. However, what neither I nor the church had fully grasped was that bringing the church back to life did not mean returning to the good old days. What it took to fill a church in 1940 did not work in 1982. I don't think anybody realized that some major things would have to be changed, added and rearranged before the hallelujah could return. This is where the unraveling began.

At first, history was a help because it gave me something to base my new programs upon. If I could find a precedent in history like the radio broadcast of the 1940's, then I could more easily institute a radio broadcast in the 1980's. After a short while though, the history began to become a hurdle. For, whenever I wanted to do something that had never been done before, such as introduce drums into Sunday morning worship, I would invariably hear those famous and fated seven last words: "We've never done it that way before!"

In the end the history was used to hang me when the majority of the members of the church voted to build a new church and move from the very location where all the history had taken place.

As quiet as it is kept, there are many churches in America which have a great deal of history, but have lost their hallelujah. Every major city has at least one. Some churches have a lot of history and have never had a hallelujah to lose. This does not mean that you cannot have both. There are several good examples of churches with both history and hallelujah.

When I say hallelujah I am not necessarily referring to using instruments other than the pipe organ in the worship, or to the denominational slant of the church. What I am talking about has more to do with the atmosphere of praise and thanksgiving and the attitude of praise which is present in the worship, ministry and life of a church, no matter what its style.

It is just that too many traditional churches think that history alone can save and satisfy the person who is seeking to grow in Christ. But, the people of today say bottom line is, “Now that you have impressed me, feed me and teach me. Make me feel the presence of the Lord. Don't bore me to death and then expect me to voluntarily come back for more!”

Some of you who may still be in the dark and don’t get it. Let me, therefore, attempt to answer what may be your unuttered, obvious question. “How, do you know when a church is losing, or has lost its hallelujah?

You know that a church has lost its hallelujah when:

- You never hear anybody say: “Hallelujah!”

- Deacons are more concerned with their dignity than their discipleship.

- Trustees are more eager to count money than to give it.

- You never hear a baby cry because there are none in the building.

- Maintenance of the facility becomes more important than the expansion of the ministry.

- Ritual and routine in worship becomes a religious rut.

- The church's rostrum is reverenced, but has heard no recent revelation.

- Church talk is more about its hey day (in the yesterday) than its active ministry today.

- Ushers look more like prison guards determined to keep the peace than hosts eager to put you at peace.

- The choir sings: " I've been running for Jesus a long time and I'm not tired yet", but they surely sound like they are tired.

- People used to have to rush to church to get a seat, now they can pick their own pew.

- Missionary work is done more indirectly by checks to surrogate providers than directly by the missionaries of the membership.

- The church feels more like a corporation than a congregation.

- Members are more concerned with who a person's mother is than who their heavenly Father is.

- The people are more concerned with where their members live than how they live.

- The bulletin becomes the script for the church, the pastor and the Holy Ghost - from which none of the above may depart.

- Sermon time becomes siesta time.

- The only celebration in the church breaks out when church is over.

If several of these signs are characteristic of your church, then maybe your church has lost its hallelujah. For, when a church has its hallelujah there is:

- Visible and audible joy in the worship;

- Space provided for the Holy Spirit to speak and reign;

- Anticipation of something new and different each Sunday;
- A sense of celebration such that worship is fun and not work;
- A warmth in the fellowship which succors members and sucks in strangers;
- A pulpit on fire with positive and prophetic proclamation;
- Music which exhorts and gives access into the presence of God;
- A congregation which is not just going, but growing and glowing for the Lord;
- An anointing on the ministry which is visible to others beside the members of the church;
- Leadership in the church which is more led by the Holy Spirit than by tradition;
- A positive pride where people are proud to be a part of that church and are willing to sacrifice for it.

By now you may be wondering, "If all of these things are true and if I have come to the conclusion that my church has or is in jeopardy of losing its hallelujah, how does a church get the hallelujah to return?" Here are several suggestions:

1. ***Admit that it is gone.*** The worse thing you can do is to act as if nothing is wrong when everything in and around your ministry is dying.

2. ***Desire to have it back.*** The honest appraisal that the hallelujah has gone is not enough to make it return. There must be a nucleus of people in the church who miss it and want it back.

3. ***Give priority to praising the Lord, not your own history.*** Remember, *hallelujah* is Hebrew for *Praise the Lord*. Therefore, even if you get a packed church and you don't praise the Lord, you will have a full house, but not a house full of hallelujah.

4. ***Plan ministry projects which challenge the people and once accomplished provide a reason for celebration.*** Just as good meat makes great gravy, churches involved in meaningful ministry automatically give off an air which can be the substance of hallelujah in a church.

5. ***Seek fresh ways to do the same things.*** The gospel is not new, nor is ministry. However, if every week the choirs sing the same songs, the deacon prays the same prayer, the preacher preaches the same sermon, worship becomes routine and stale. Don't be a heretic or an entertainer, but be creative as you worship, praise and serve the Lord.

6. ***Change order of worship every now and then.*** This suggestion is in some ways a part of the previous one. Do something different. You might even want to do something I did once and gave almost everybody in the church a heart attack. I had the secretary print up covers of the weekly church bulletin and it was completely blank inside. We passed them out in an effort to point out that we get so caught up in our order of worship that we leave no space for the Spirit to operate. At the church I serve now, we don't have a weekly church bulletin to outline the worship. We have learned to go with the flow!

7. ***Sensitize the church to the goodness of the Lord.*** There is no way that a people who know how good the Lord has been to them can withhold their praise from Him. Maybe we should talk less about the headlines of Time Magazine and Newsweek and focus more on the highlights of God's goodness to us.

8. ***Serve people.*** When the needs of people become the focus of your church and meeting those needs become the purpose for each of your church's ministries, then you will not have to worry about attracting crowds or ever hearing hallelujah. People flock to the place where their needs are met.

From Mission To Mausoleum

When Mary came running to the tomb of Jesus on that first Resurrection Sunday morning, she was distraught to discover that Jesus was not there. She met an angel who asked her a question which he still asks today, *"Why seek ye the living among the dead?"*

In Mary's case, at least she was in a cemetery where the dead should be found. Her problem was that she just did not know Jesus had risen. In the case of far too many churches, whose sanctuaries have become cemeteries, the same angel sits upon the front door and still asks those who enter looking for the Lord and for life, *"Why seek ye the living among the dead?"*

Even today the angel says: "Can't you tell that the living Lord whom you seek is not here? Don't you see that the everlasting life which you desire is not here. Haven't you been able to pick up on the fact that the life which should characterize the church is not here. What does it take for you to see that the reason that you do not see Christ is because this church has died and he is not here!"

Believe me, there is no death sadder than the death of a church. And churches are dying by the hundreds every-day. Many of them are already dead, their caskets continue to be open for viewing and their remains await only the public funeral and final burial. Let me give you an example.

There was a predominately white Baptist church in a New England urban area. This church used to be a thriving center of Christian celebration, education and service. Then, as is often the case, its neighborhood began to change. First, the blacks moved in. Then, right behind them came the Hispanics. It wasn't long before all the members of the white church moved away with no intention of ever returning, even to go to church. This left their church building a towering tombstone to mark the spot where their church had died.

Think of it. This church was a city block long. It had a gymnasium, a built in pipe organ and several baby grand pianos. Its educational wing was equipped with church school classrooms, offices and a fellowship hall. It was completely paid for with an endowment in the bank. Its main sanctuary seated 1000 people. And yet, in its last days only 18 senior citizens attended worship on communion Sunday. Each week, the faithful who remained, assembled themselves together like family members gather at a grave on Memorial Day, as if only to pay their respects to the dearly departed.

The place that was a home away from home had become an abandoned house. The place which was once filled with merriment was now a place filled with mourning. The place of liveliness had become the place of lifelessness. The place where one would hear the sound of babies crying was the place where arthritic bones were now cracking. The place which once had wall to wall people, now only had wall to wall pews. The place where bouncing basketballs could be heard in the gym was the place where the only things to be heard were the echoes of hollow hymns bouncing off the walls. The place where the smell of food cooking in the fellowship hall had been replaced by the smell of mildew in the sanctuary. What once had been an active ministry had become a mausoleum.

How does this happen? Churches which have become mausoleums don't get that way all at once. Most churches do not die instantly of heart attacks. They die slowly over time. In fact, one might even describe the life of a dying church as one which may begin in its initial mission phase and if not checked can progress toward certain death.

A Mission Church

There is a whole denomination of Baptists who insist on having the word "missionary" in the name of their church. However, when one analyzes some of their actions, it is clear that *mission* could hardly be further from their minds. When I speak of mission, I am not talking about how much money is allocated in the budget to spend on it. Nor am I referring to how many bulletin boards are filled with maps of foreign mission fields.

A mission church could be a church of any age, any size and located anywhere but which: 1. has a clear sense of being on a mission (It has a clear sense of purpose.); 2. is itself a mission (It is a place where people are ministered to and served.); and 3. produces multiplied numbers of missionaries (Members are actually equipped, empowered and sent forth to minister).

When most churches begin, they begin with a sense of mission. They have a consciousness that they have been called specifically and especially for a unique divine purpose. They pursue it with passion, godly pride and power. They are excited and this excitement about being sent is contagious. It may be driven by a desire to make disciples for Christ. It may be motivated by a compassion for those in pain. It may be fueled by a fiery love for the lost. It may even be nudged along by a need to prove a point. Whatever the force behind it, a mission church is a church where both minister and members are clear on why they exist. A mission church is able to point to specific tasks it has been called to do and visible signs of the fruits of its labors.

The members of a mission church can't wait for Sunday to come because that is when they can celebrate what they have been doing for the Lord the other six days. This church doesn't need a missionary department because every member sees themselves as a missionary. This church does not require a uniform to identify the missionaries because they are known in the church and in the community by their deeds, not their dress.

These folk don't have to be publicly authorized to serve because they have already been commissioned by Christ. This church does not need missionary circles because every person's sphere of influence becomes their own personal missionary circle. This church may believe in continuing education, but it does not spend more time in workshops than in witnessing. Nor, does it place more emphasis on attending conventions about mission than actually carrying out mission.

A mission church does not only have a sense of being called. It is also a church which is itself a mission.

That is to say, it is not only a place from which people are sent. It is also a place to which people are sent. Its sense of calling and seriousness about it purpose becomes a matter of fact in the community which it serves. The mission church functions in its environment as a mission station to which those in need are referred and fed.

When a church is a mission, it figuratively and literally becomes a lighthouse for the lost; a way station for the wayward; a refuge for the rejected; an outpost for the outcast; and a pit stop for weary runners in the rat race of life.

Thirdly, mission churches are characterized by the mass production of missionaries. In these churches, it seems like everyone there is a missionary on a mission. Interestingly enough, they are not missionaries by training, but missionaries by transformation. That is to say, like the woman whom Jesus met at the well, they immediately run and tell what happened to them when they met Jesus. They may not know the four spiritual laws, or formulas for salvation. They just knew and tell what the Lord has done for them.

What happens in mission churches is so exciting and life changing that everyone who touches them leaves there testifying and thereby a missionary. Some leave with a specific message and witness, or purpose. Others leave with a personal testimony about what happened to them when they met Jesus there. Then, still others who may not have met Jesus leave with a testimony of the intensity of the Christianity to be found there. Thus, they do not make so many witnesses because they teach people to witness. They do so because what happens to people in such churches is the kind of thing that you might say you are not going to tell anybody, but discover that you just can't keep it to yourself!

It takes a special kind of person to minister to and lead a mission church. The principle characterization of the pastor of a mission church is that of pioneer. This pastor must fearlessly go where none have gone before; serve those whom none have served before; attempt what none has ever tried before; do what none has ever done before. This pastor and the people who are drawn to him or her are pioneers.

A Ministry Church

This excitement and unbridled zeal cannot last forever. And it does not. For after churches past through the mission church phase they begin to become a ministry church. In the mission church phase they go forth, but in the ministry church phase they begin to establish.

It is in this phase that they put together their structure and become institutionalized. It is here that they develop auxiliaries, organizations, clubs, rules, regulations and systems for the delivery of services. A ministry church is a natural and, to a degree, necessary progression from the mission church because without organization and structure, the mission church would soon burn itself up.

The problem, however, with churches in this ministry church phase is that they tend to behave more like organizations than organisms. Obviously, there are degrees, but in these churches, there is a place for everybody and a time for everything. They run like well oiled machines.

The pastor best suited for a ministry church is one who is a good manager and administrator! The pastor's primary job in this type of church is to keep all systems functioning properly. This pastor does not need to be so much of a pioneer as in the case of the mission church pastor. The pastor of the ministry church must creatively establish, manage and expand what has already been begun.

A Museum Church

Our prayer is that every church could sustain itself in the mission phase, the ministry phase or a combination of the two. However, unfortunately this is not always the case. For some church move beyond the ministry church phase to what I call the museum church phase. In this phase, the sense of purpose found in the mission church is gone. The vibrant organized activity of the ministry church is gone. These have been replaced by a well documented memory of what used to be.

When you visit a mission church you feel the fire of praise and worship. When you visit a ministry church you hear the hum of activity. When you visit a museum church, you see the artifacts of the exploits of yesteryear and by gone days.

In a museum the church, the living enter in order to tour the place. The whole energy of the church is used up in pointing to pictures, plaques and people of former glory.

Visitors and new members are shown what they missed, not what they can expect to have. As a new member of a museum church you get the sense of joining history which you really can't join because you came along too late.

Here, historical artifacts gain in importance over the urgency of ministry. The whole church is like a living room where no one is allowed to sit on the sofa! In these churches, all you hear is: “You can’t touch that.” “Don’t sit there!” and “Remember when?”

The pastor of the museum church is essentially a curator and tour guide! All he, or she must be able to do is preserve the artifacts, remember and recite their significance upon demand and be able to show others around every now and then. This preacher is expected to pay more attention to the church’s history, than *His* story!

A Mausoleum Church

In a museum church, people come to see the ministerial artifacts which have been left by a once vibrant congregation. In a mausoleum church, the living don't come for a tour of remaining objects. Instead, they are forced to actually keep company with the dead.

Once a church has gotten to this stage, the only reason to come to it is to pay your last respects. Mausoleum churches are where dead saints “live.” They are walking around. They are breathing. They are in good physical health, but for all practical purposes they are spiritually dead. The worship is dead. The preaching is dead. The singing is dead. The ministry is dead. The fellowship is dead. And even their hope is dead.

The pastor of this church is a caretaker. All he, or she does is visit the sick who are about to die; bury the dead who have just died; and attempt to beautify a building which like a white washed sepulchre houses the dead. The only hope for such a church is to do to it what Jesus did for Lazarus. Stand before it and in the name of Jesus Christ command it to come forth!

The value of this typology of churches is that it becomes a useful tool in helping preachers know what kind of churches they want to accept as pastors and it also helps churches to know what type of preachers they need to call as pastors.

If, for example, a church is content where they are and with what they are, in order to maintain the status quo a mission church must have a pioneering prophet. A ministry church must have a manager. A museum church must have a tour guide and a mausoluem church must have a caretaker.

If, on the other hand, a church is not satisfied with where and what they are, maybe they should consider calling a pastor who has the qualities best suited for the kind of church they would like to be. That is to say, if the zeal in a mission church has gone out of control, maybe they need a manager. If a ministry church, a museum church, or a mausoleum church has become too routine or just plain dead, maybe they should consider calling a pioneering prophet.

The point is that the type of church yours becomes is directly related to the type of leadership it has and is willing to follow.

Wherever your church may be in this scheme of things, make sure that in it, you do whatever is necessary to keep the fires of the missionary church burning, keep the activity of the ministry church going and, as much as you can, avoid the death and dying so characteristic of the museum and mausoleum churches.

By-Laws Over the Bible

Years ago, we had a deacon in our church who used to say he heard Dr. Gardner Taylor remark: *"Man's laws and by-laws are 'bout to out law, God's laws."* Then, this deacon would invariably reach into his pocket and produce a miniature copy of the church's by-laws and proceed to quote the by-laws to me chapter and verse just like he was reciting scripture!

What is it with church by-laws these days? It seems that they have been elevated to a status which rivals divine revelation. They have been given an authority which heretofore had only been reserved for the law of God. They are being cited more than scripture. They are being referred to more than the Bible. How is it that church folk today are now giving more weight to their own by-laws than to the Bible?

If you will indulge this somewhat unscientific response, I believe we can identify several reasons for this. In the first place, church folk are giving by-laws more weight than the Bible because ***many of them don't read the Bible***. Despite our rhetoric about the Bible being the word of God, our daily bread, a lamp unto our feet and a light unto our pathway, many Christians go for days, weeks, and even months without reading the word of God. The only scripture they read is that which they read or hear in church. When a person does not read the word of God on a regular basis, they cannot know how their church's by-laws stack up to it. Because many church folk know their by-laws better than the Bible, they simply go with what they know.

Secondly, it might be said that many church folk give more weight to their by-laws than the Bible because ***they don't believe the Bible***. Now, this sounds extremely strange, but to many people active in the church today, the Bible is a book of fantastic stories which are too incredible to be believed or applied to their own lives. After all, what God did for Moses, Daniel, Shadrach, Meshach and Abednego was then, this is now. If we do not believe that the things in the Bible ever happened or that they are God's word to us here and now, how can we be serious about doing what they say?

Thirdly, many church folk give more weight to their own by-laws than the Bible because ***they don't want to follow the Bible***. Here, the problem is not ignorance. These "Christians" know what the Bible says, they believe that the Bible is right, but the truth is too inconvenient or uncomfortable for them to follow. They are inclined to say like a deacon told me once when I shared with him what scripture said concerning a certain issue that had risen in the church: “We don’t care what the Bible says, we ain’t gonna change!”

Then, lastly, we might note that some church folk give more weight to their by-laws than the Bible because ***they simply refuse to be judged by the Bible***. For them, the Bible has become a window out of which they may criticize the world and not a mirror in which they can see themselves. By-laws are favored because they justify us while the bible tends to judge us.

Thus, for these reasons and perhaps many more, our churches are bogged down in battles between by-laws and the Bible. More often than not, the by-laws win! As a matter of fact, not only are there those who give more weight to by-laws than the Bible, but for them, by-laws are actually better than the Bible. Here are some of the reasons why.

By-laws are better than the Bible because ***since we make up our own by-laws, we can understand them.*** We do not have to learn another language or dig through dictionaries, concordances and commentaries to understand what they mean. If they say, there must be seven trustees on the church board, elected each year on the Monday after the third Sunday, we can understand that.

By-laws are better than the Bible because ***they speak specifically to our church situation.*** These rules were written directly for this church body and outline how ours should be run. Even though some by-laws are themselves out dated, many members still prefer them over the word because of their direct and obvious connection to their church's history.

By-laws are better than the Bible because ***we can add to, subtract from or change our own by-laws at will.*** We can't do that with the Bible. If we don't like something in the Bible, the most we can do is just ignore it. If we don't like something in our by-laws all we have to is just change it.

By-laws are better than the Bible because ***they are short enough to master.*** Granted, some church by-laws are fairly thick and detailed, but for the most part, they are not sixty-six books spanning several thousand years. Most people can master and even memorize a set of by-laws a lot quicker than they can remember and retain the whole counsel of God.

By-laws are better than the Bible because ***they derive their authority from the fact that we agree upon them, not because they have been imposed upon us from some external source.*** Our laws are more palatable because they are not revealed to us from on high, they are handed up to us from "down low!"

By-laws are better than the Bible because ***we can regulate our own interpretation of what the by-laws means.*** If we do not like what a given article in the by-laws says, we can not only change it, but we can even legislate how it is to be interpreted. Not, so with the Bible. Christians have been falling out for centuries over how to interpret the Bible. Chances are they will continue to do so.

Having said all of this about the over emphasis that our churches are tending to place on their own by-laws, let me close with a few reasons why we must return our focus to the bible. Whenever and wherever there is conflict between the two there should be no question, we must place God's word over own by-laws.

When we place the Bible over by-laws, ***we tend to shift the focus from what we want to what God wants.*** Let us not forget the purpose of the church and the meaning of discipleship. Both we and the church belong to God. As such, He has a right to regulate how we behave and what we are bound to do. When faced with painful obedience His own son, Jesus Christ gave us a model by saying: "Not my will, but Thine be done."

When we place the Bible over by-laws ***we tend to put biblical principles and practices over personal preferences.*** Needless to say, there are many things which I would rather do. However, just because I prefer them, does not make them right, or biblically sound. The written word (bible) and the living word (Jesus Christ) are the foundations of the church, not what we think, or desire. The song writer Edward Mote voiced my sentiments exactly when he wrote: *"My hope is built on nothing less than Jesus blood and righteousness, I dare not trust the sweetest frame, but wholly lean on Jesus name. On Christ the solid rock I stand all other ground is sinking sand., All other ground is sinking sand."*

When we place the Bible over by-laws, ***we learn to conform to that which does not change, versus always seeking to change that which we do not like.*** The virtue of scripture is that throughout the changing ages, it remains the same. Indeed, Jesus said that heaven and earth will pass away, but His word would stand forever. Instead of trying to be hip and with the latest fad, we should seek to anchor ourselves to the Lord's word.

When we place the bible over by-laws, ***we learn to give space for the Holy Spirit to work.*** It is true. The letter (and the law) killeth, but the spirit maketh alive. The same Holy Spirit who inspired the original writers of scripture is still available to interpret it to present day readers of scripture. When we give the Spirit space, He will not only reveal to us the meaning of the ancient word, but show us its appropriate application to our church and personal lives.

When we place the Bible over by-laws, ***we learn to seek God's guidance and counsel in it and through it rather than ourselves.*** The whole point here is that this love affair that many church folk have with their by-laws is nothing other than idolatry. They have given the devotion, attention, and love of God to some thing other than God. Jesus said it well when He said: *"Seek ye first the kingdom of God and His righteousness; and all these things shall be added unto you."*

Surely, the house of God should have rules, regulations and guidelines. Any other way would be chaos and confusion. God is not the author of confusion. In His house everything should be done in decency and order. However, inasmuch as it is His house, His laws ought to take priority over ours.

One Pastor - Four Churches

Not once in all my twenty some years of pastoring, have I ever received four salaries, four parsonages, four cars, four anniversaries or four pensions from the same church! Here's what I mean.

When I was called to each of the two churches I served, I discovered it's not "what you see is what you get," but "what you *don't* see it what you get." As the pastor of *one* church, I always found myself having to deal with at least *four* churches within that church. This caused me to perform a daily balancing act which required great skill and divine guidance.

I was responsible for and accountable to each of these four churches and was expected to serve each in such a way that I attended to its specific needs while not neglecting the needs of the others.

My first church was the church of the nursery. This church is the church that keeps the rest of the church visionary. This was the church comprised of the babies crying in the church nursery, as well as, unborn babies on their way. This church was not really here yet, but if we wanted to have a church in twenty years, there were some things that we had to do now to prepare for them. The members of the church of the nursery require space in your facility, age specific ministry and high priority.

The church of the nursery is easy to plan for, but politically difficult to fight for. Many church people can't stand the sound of babies crying in worship, not to mention the creation of ministries which place a priority on children and youth. I often found myself fighting for the needs of members who had not yet learned how to walk, or had not even been born.

A simple example would be whether, or not to turn an adult classroom in the church's lower auditorium into a nursery. *"Well, we've been in that classroom since 1942, why should we move?"*

I have learned that my responsibility as the pastor of the church of the nursery is to prepare for this crowd. For, if we are blessed, they will be coming!

The second church which I had to pastor, whether I liked it or not, was the church of the cemetery. This church keeps the church anchored. I have been the pastor of two churches which were 100 years old or more. Such churches have a considerable congregation in the cemetery.

These dearly departed members are physically absent, but mightily present in the pictures which hang on the church walls, the engravings on the stained glass windows, the plaques strategically placed throughout the church, the names above various rooms, the legends about their exploits and the offspring which they have left behind.

At first I could not believe how much clout dead people could have. I had become the pastor of ghosts! "Though being dead, they yet speaketh!" I shall never forget asking an associate preacher of mine why he was so adamantly opposed to a program I was proposing for the church. You will not believe what he said. "On behalf of my mother who is sleeping in her grave!" I could not believe it. This man was fighting me tooth and nail because of what he thought his mother who had been dead for years might think.

Never underestimate this cemetery congregation. If you honor them, they can help you, but if you ignore and disrespect them, you might end up joining them. If you are a young pastor, or a new pastor going to a church, make sure that in addition to the pulpit committee, you have someone introduce you to the cemetery crowd.

My third church was the church of the sanctuary. This crowd kept the church active and alive. This is the crowd which most people think of as the church. This is the crowd that is present on Sunday mornings. You see them on a regular basis.

This is the crowd that is paying. Unlike the babies in the nursery, or the dead in the cemetery, this crowd is the one that pays the church bills through their tithes and offerings. This is the crowd that participates in the various church ministries. And this is the crowd that is the most political.

Because it is present, paying, participating and political, this crowd requires great attention. For, if they are not properly tended to, all of the other churches might fall apart. Yet, if they are catered to, to the exclusion of the others, your whole church may fall apart in a matter of a few short years.

As a pastor, I must feed this sanctuary crowd. Feed them the word. Feed them the vision. Feed them a vehicle for reaching the vision. Feed them understanding of how they stand between the nursery and the cemetery. They are the ones who must honor the dead with their decisions while preparing for the unborn with their dollars.

The last church which I pastored was the church of the community. This "community church" kept the sanctuary church honest and growing. This is the crowd that does not technically belong to my church, but which lives in the sphere of my church's ministry. This includes other churches, neighbors of the church, potential members of the church, visitors to the church, community groups, our radio and television audience, government officials, and even perpetual critics of me and my church.

Even though these people do not belong to your church, what you do inside of your church will get back to them and in many ways may effect them. It is often a tough call to lead your sanctuary church to do things which place the needs of the community church over theirs. I have gotten into trouble for this many times. *"Reverend why are you spending so much time out there with those people? We are the one's paying your salary?"*

What is not being understood by these isolationist saints is that the church does not exist in a vacuum. Furthermore, it was never designed to be a cocoon. It was supposed to be an outpost from which the saints of God would for forth into all the world. As the pastor of the church of the community, I must serve this crowd as well.

Each of these four churches has its place and each takes its turn in the spotlight. However, any church which plans to be around for any length of time must learn how to balance, blend and bless them all under *one* roof as *one* church.

Entering into the Wrong Courts

David talked about God's people entering courts. However, he said enter *God's courts with thanksgiving.* He did not hardly mean that we should enter *secular courts with misgivings.* Yet, that is precisely what more and more church members are doing everyday. Sisters and brothers in Christ have become plaintiffs and defendants in court.

As a result, our prayers have become political, our praise has become non-existent, our camaraderie has been killed and our sermons have to be preached under security. Going to church under the auspices of the court becomes a mere exercise in going through the motions.

Going to court to settle church disputes is frowned upon by the Bible. It is warned against by Jesus (Matthew 5:25-26). It is called a shame by Paul. (I Corinthians 6:1-6). And based on the experience of one who has been there, it undermines trust and authority in the church just as divorce does in marriage.

Usually, by the time a church gets to court, the damage has already been done. What's left for the judge to do is merely a matter of how to deal with the damage and disperse the wreckage.

Nevertheless, this does not stop church folk from going to court. They go to court to: remove pastors, settle property rights, expel members, establish governing rights, prosecute dishonest ministers and leaders and any other little thing you can imagine.

So, why then are so many churches in court today? There are several reasons for this.

So many churches are in court today because we are creatures of our culture and we live in a litigious society. People will sue you today for just about anything. The people of God are no different. We have become the litigious religious.

So many churches are in court today because we have been so blessed that we can now afford to hire lawyers. There was a time that we prayed through our problems because that was all we could afford! Now that affluence has begun to attend church, church folk can take their burdens to the lawyer instead of to the Lord!

So many churches are in court today because we have the wrong model of what the church is. Instead of a model of family or community, the model for the church is corporation, social organization and/or club. Where these models are lifted, rules, by-laws and business may very easily take precedence over revelation, forgiveness, forbearance and love.

So many churches are in court today because many of them have become so large (in fact or in spirit) that the members relate to each other through the laws of the church and the law of the land more so that through rich and real personal relationships. The old adage is right. "Rules without relationship leads to rebellion." People who know and love each other tend to solve interpersonal problems differently than total strangers.

So many churches are in court today because we have forgotten that the church belongs to the Lord. Look at us! Here we are in man's court fighting over God's stuff! Since it all belongs to Him. Our disputes ought to be settled by Him.

Despite the fact that churches are in court, what they are finding is that there are certain things that a secular court cannot do.

A secular court can rule on a dispute, but it cannot settle an argument. Even after the judge rules on a matter, animosity and enmity still exists. It's not over just because the judge has made a ruling.

A secular court cannot heal wounded hearts. Much of what brings church folk to court in the first place are hurts which have been inflicted and felt at the level of the heart. Judges may be legal authorities, but they are by no means heart specialists.

A secular court cannot legislate love. In I Corinthians 13 when Paul mentions faith, hope and love, he sites that the greatest of these is love. The reason this is true is because love can do what laws cannot. Judges can force us to stick to the letter of the law, but only God can make us willingly want to practice the demands of love.

A secular court cannot force people of faith to have faith. Often, churches find themselves in court at odds over matters of faith. By this, I do not mean to say that they are they wrestling with doctrinal issues. Rather, they disagree over *visions* which can only be seen by faith; *leadership* which can only be submitted to by faith; *property* which can only be acquired by faith; and *peace* and *harmony* which can only claimed by faith.

A secular court cannot sentence us to be sensitive and self-sacrificing saints. The bottom line is that courts cannot make us act like Christians. It would be nice though if they could. What Jesus told Nicodemus that night is still true. If we are ever to be the church which God has called us to be, we must be born again!

All of this ranting and raving about the evils of going to court does not erase the fact that church people will inevitably find themselves in conflict. How then, are we to settle disputes if we are not to take them to court? Scripture offers us several models which we might implement.

Abraham and Lot

The Lord had prospered Abraham and his nephew Lot so much that their cattle and herds began to intermingle. This caused their herdsmen to fight and constantly be at odds. When the issue was raised, the gracious and generous Abraham said to Lot: "Let there be no strife between us for we are brothers. The whole land is before us. If you go to the left, I will go to the right. If you go to the right, I will go to the left." This dispute was settled because the two parties were able to separate in peace and love.

Jesus in Matthew 18

In Matthew 18:15-20, Jesus sets forth what might be thought of as the rules of Christian conflict management. Here, Jesus tells us what to do when there is a dispute between Christians. Step one is to go to that person, privately with the concern. If that does not work, step two is to take one or two with you and attempt to resolve the matter. If that doesn't work, then, said Jesus, tell it to the church (or designated representatives of the church). Jesus says, if they will not hear the church, then let them be unto you as a heathen and a publican. In other words, once the church itself has spoken, that is it. There is no higher court because the Lord goes on to say that whatsoever *we* shall bind on earth shall be bound in heaven and whatsoever *we* shall loose on earth shall be loosed in heaven.

The Apostles and the Widows

In Acts 6, we read about the tremendous growth of the early church and a major murmuring that arose as a result. It seems that there was a certain group of Greek speaking widows who felt that they were not getting as much food, or attention as their Hebrew counterparts. Therefore, they began to mumble and murmur about it.

Instead of the church dividing over the matter, the wise apostles *created a ministry* to address the problem. Deacons came into being to help the apostles (pastors) carry the load of meeting the needs of the people. The bible says that after this ministry was created to meet the need, the church grew even more. This model tells us to stop mumbling and start ministering!

Paul's Method

Like Jesus, Paul too, believed in the authority of the church to settle its own disputes. He writes about this to the Corinthians in I Corinthians 6:1-11. Basically, Paul says that we have no business taking our business before secular courts, when at the end of time we shall be given authority to judge angels. This part is not new. What Paul offers here as a suggestion for the resolution of church conflict is a tough pill for some people to swallow. That is, he suggests that we rather just let it go and be offended than to destroy each other and the church in the process. "Why do ye not rather take wrong? Why do ye not rather yourselves to be defrauded? Nay, ye do wrong and defraud, and that even your brethren." (I Corinthians 6:7-8) What we hear in the church sounds more like this: "Don't they know who I am? I ain't gotta take that!" - And we don't!

King Solomon in I Kings 3:16-27 provides us with a similar example of settling a conflict with sacrifice when he suggests to two women fighting over a baby that the baby be cut in two so that both could have their share. The real mother chose to give up her rights to the baby just so that it would continue to live. In this way she won the baby back because Solomon knew that only real love could sacrifice in this way.

Peter and Cornelius

Although he had been converted, we know that Peter still held certain prejudices in his heart against Gentiles. These feelings were based on centuries of Jewish belief and practice. However, we read about it being set aside in Acts 10 when the Lord showed him a vision and prepared him to go to the house of a certain gentile named Cornelius. When Peter got there, he found an eagerness on the Gentiles' part to hear the word about Jesus. Furthermore, the Holy Spirit fell on them while he preached. This age old enmity between Peter and the Gentiles was settled for him by his willingness to be open to the leading and guiding of the Spirit.

When we attempt to settle something, it may well rise again. When the Spirit settles a matter, you had better believe it's over!

The Stressosphere

The gaseous substance which surrounds the earth is called the atmosphere. This atmosphere extends far into outer space and is itself made up of several spheres. Nearest to the earth and up to about seven miles above sea level is the troposphere. From seven miles to about 30 miles above sea level is the stratosphere. Thirty to fifty miles above sea level is the mesosphere. More than seventy five miles above sea level is the thermosphere. One thousand miles from earth is the magnetosphere.

You may remember all of these names from high school physics. However, there is another sphere which we all know but have never named. It is much closer to home. It is called the stressosphere.

I first discovered the stressophere when I noticed that whenever I left the city where I served as pastor, I could literally and physically feel a weight and heaviness leave my body. While I was away, I felt traces of the stressophere in my hotel room when I called the church for my messages. Then, upon my return, especially when flying, just before the pilot would announce that we were twenty minutes from landing, I felt the weight of the stressosphere overcome me.

Paul was on to something when he spoke of "the care of the churches." I have no scientific proof to verify the parameters or coordinates of the stressosphere, but as sure as I am alive, I know that there is one.

This is not the stress which we carry with us. It is the stress tied to an environment which brings on stress. For me, that place had become the church of which I had been the pastor for several years. Like a constant cloud, it hovered over the place. Like a foul odor, it was all throughout the place. Like a dome with doors, it encompassed the place. Like a magnetic force field, it emanated from the place.

This was not simply the stress of meeting deadlines, being over worked, or even being burned out. All of these are normal by products of a busy and productive life. When I say that my church had become a stressosphere, I mean something deeper than this.

When I was first called to that church, I could not wait to get there. I would be at home wishing I were there. My mind was always there. My thoughts were always there. My heart was always there. My future was always there. But, then after countless crucifixions, what seemed like a million meaningless meetings, and all out war, that building began to be associated with the pain which I had so often experienced inside of it.

The same was true for my children. They used to cheer when they saw the church from the expressway as we approached it. The deaconesses used to keep them there during the day. They literally grew up there. They had toys and a crib there. (That's because my wife was having her stressophere at home due to two little ones, two larger ones and me!) However, towards the end their cry was: "Do we have to go there!"

The church that used to be a haven was now hell. The sanctuary which used to be the site of support and celebration was now associated with my own suffering. The altar on which prayers were offered was now the place where my character, dreams and integrity had nearly been slain. The pulpit from which I had so boldly proclaimed the gospel became the bulls eye at which potshots were thrown at me.

The parking lot which used to overflow with cars, now had the cars along with impromptu meetings after church meetings. The restrooms which were designed for rest became the mouth for a river of rumors. The prayer meeting which was created for people to talk to God, became the time when they talked about me. The hallowed halls which had been walked by great saints, were now the hideouts for huddled cliques. Many of the people who once considered themselves family had now become the adversary.

Somehow, by the grace of God, I was always able to function because I had learned to live with it like a diabetic lives with insulin needles or a person with emphysema lives with an oxygen tank. Just because they are necessary to make it, does not mean you have to like it. In fact, I didn't. I hated it.

Going to worship had become worse than going to work. It is hard to serve in a church where you are the pastor, and *you* can't wait for the benediction so that you can hurry up and get out of the church.

The stressophere did not come upon me all at once. In the beginning, it was only associated with the city. Then, the area. Then, the neighborhood of the church. Then, the parking lot. Then, the building. Then, the board room. Then, my office. Then, the sanctuary. And finally, the pulpit.

The closer I got to the church, the more I would feel it. I would feel it on the expressway. I would feel it in certain rooms. I would feel it just before certain meetings. Once, I remember coming into the board room late and it seemed that they were all waiting for me because I was not only the topic of discussion, but the main course for dinner. They always saved my seat, and believe me, when I came in the room I was often afraid to sit in it.

I would feel it whenever I came near certain people. I could feel it when I thought about certain subjects. People other than me felt it. Members felt it. Visitors felt it. It was there.

Up to that point, the pulpit was the only place I felt free. Then, one Sunday, while sitting in the pulpit, I was struck by the stressosphere. I looked to my right and saw choir members who were conspiring to sue me. I looked behind me in the pulpit and saw associate preachers who had revolted against me. I looked just ahead and saw deacons who wished they could fire me.

I looked to the rear and witnessed members in the alcove tape recording me. I looked in the aisles and saw a faithful foe walking out on me. I looked to my left and saw officers who were clearly not for me. Then, I looked at the communion table at which I was supposed to serve in sincerity! Oh, no! The stressophere!

Where did the stress come from? It came from constant conflict over the mission of the church and the methods by which it should be manifested. It came from memories of mistreatment and misbehavior. It came from dishonesty and hypocrisy which paraded around in sanctified garments. It came from a sense of powerlessness to do anything about it.

Perhaps, you have experienced the stressophere in your situation and know what I mean. If the Lord doesn't help you through it, it can be unbearable. How does a person survive it? How does one deal with it?

1. ***Confess it.*** Be real and stop trying to call it everything but what it is. You are not simply tired and in need of a vacation. It is not the asbestos in the ceiling or the lead paint on the wall. There is a serious presence in the place(s) you serve which makes you feel extremely tense and uncomfortable. It's okay. You don't have to be cool.

2. ***Confront it.*** The next step is to confront it and the people or issues which cause it. This confrontation may take the form of talking with individual people, meeting with groups of people, or even raising and attempting to resolve stressful matters through systematic and professional means (e.g. mediation and/or counseling).

3. ***Convert it.*** Sometimes, you will find that no manner of confrontation will erase or eradicate the stressophere. This is when you must learn how to convert that stress into strength. As amazing as it may sound, the stress that you are now feeling in the place you serve can become a spiritual radar to warn you when danger is near and to prepare you for the attack of the enemy.

4. ***Compare it, keep it in perspective.*** In your honest assessment of your situation you may not only be forced to confess the existence of a stressophere in your life. You may also have to admit that it is not nearly as bad as you are making it out to be. When you keep your burdens and blessings in perspective, you often see that it is not the problem that is so bad. It is your reaction to the problem.

5. ***Turn it over.*** Just as God is the only one that could create the atmosphere, God is the only one that can completely remove the stressophere. Indeed, he made an offer to do it through his son nearly two thousand years ago. "Come unto me all ye that labor and are heavy laden and I will give your rest. Take my yoke upon you and learn of me, for my yoke is easy and my burdens are light." As we turn control of our lives over to Him, our stress, even though the people and the place may not change, God chases the stress away like

Lysol Spray covers and kills foul odors.

6. ***Leave it.*** The simplest way to deal with the stressophere is to leave it. But don't leave it until it leaves you. In other words, if you run from the stressophere to another place, it will hunt you down and move into wherever you relocate. However, if you conquer it while you are yet in it, then when you leave the site of the stressophere, *it will stay there* and never rise up to haunt or hurt you again.

Traps of Typical Preachers

" I Just Gotta Have A Church!"

Even though I began preaching at the early age of twelve, I had sense enough then to know that I never wanted to be the pastor of a church. It was obvious to my little eyes that this life was not for me. I was more inclined to receive the words of Paul to Timothy and to "do the work of an evangelist."

The evangelist didn't have to preach to the same people every week. The evangelist was always a special guest and was treated as such. The evangelist never had to deal with discipling, or disciplining, only with convicting and converting. The evangelist could love 'em and leave 'em. The evangelist didn't have to implement the implications of his preaching. The evangelist was free to be a rolling stone, sowing the seed, but gathering no moss. In other words, as I saw it then, the evangelist was a person who basically preached the gospel, won souls for Christ and that was it!

However, pastors had a completely different calling. To me, pastors had too much baggage to carry; too many burdens to bear; too many beatings to take; too many board meetings to attend; too many brawls to break up; too many bureaucrats to manage; too many backs to scratch; too much battling to do; too many babies to bless; too many bereaved to comfort; too much blame to share; too many business meetings to chair; and too many budgets to meet. Even at the tender age of twelve, I perceived that being the pastor of a church was a thankless job and I wanted no parts of it. That is, until I got bitten by the "I just gotta have a church bug!"

You mean, you have never heard of the "I just gotta have a church bug?" Well then, before I tell you how I caught it, perhaps I should tell you what it is. *The "I just gotta have a church bug" is a virus which infects the heart and soul of a preacher and causes him or her to suddenly feel empty, lonely, unworthy and a deep sense of inferiority because he, or she is not the pastor of a church.*

This is a communicable disease which is spread by preachers who treat non-pastor preachers as pions. It is kept going by parishioners who keep asking, "Don't you have a church yet?" It is made worse by the preacher's peers who are called to churches, but who have far less ability and credibility than they do.

The "I just gotta have church bug" is an obsession to be a pastor whose source is either peer pressure or pride. It has nothing to do with a high holy calling of God to minister to His people. As far as these preachers are concerned, the cure for this bug is to see their name on the bulletin of the church; have “pastor” engraved in a plaque on their office door; see a sign at the curb saying “reserved for pastor;” and/or having a regular place to preach every Sunday.

In many ways, a preacher with this bug is like a person who can't get a date. At first, they may be glad to be single and free. However, soon others who see them always alone will begin to wonder out loud whether or not there is something wrong with them. If a person is insecure about themselves, it won't be long before they will be wondering the same thing about themselves. *“What is wrong with my ministry that no one wants me. What is the matter with my preaching that no one will call me.”*

After a while, these preachers start breaking out in a cold sweat, questioning their call and sending their resumes to every vacant church in the land. Not because they want to serve God's people, but because they've just gotta get a church to satisfy their pride and prove the point that somebody wants them.

When this disease is in its severest stages, the preacher doesn't care where the church is; what the church building looks like; how many members they have; how much money they raise; how many of them are really saved; what they are going to pay him; how they are going to treat his wife and family; or what happened to the pastor before him. All he wants is to be able to say: *"I am the pastor."*

So, like a junkie looking for a hit, he searches high and low, preaches far and wide trying to find a church to call him. Some preachers have it so bad that they will do virtually anything to get called. They play politics with the people. They try to butter up the pulpit committee. They seed the parishioners with ammunition for them and against their competition. They barrage the church with recommendations. They lobby until the Lord comes. Just to get a church.

Pulpit committees perceive this disease and govern themselves accordingly. For, while there are some churches who do not want anyone who they feel nobody else wants, there are other churches who have the compatible disease. It is called the "We've just gotta have a pastor bug." This is a perfect fit for the preacher who's just gotta have a church. The church that just gotta have a pastor, doesn't care whether or not he's saved, can preach, cares about people, has any training, has any administrative skills, can teach, or has a vision.

All that matters to them is: "We've been vacant so long that the people in the city are beginning to talk, the people in the church are beginning to leave and the ministry in the church is beginning to die, so we gotta have a pastor."

You talk about a sad combination! That is a preacher who just gotta have a church and a church who's just gotta have a pastor getting together. They are a perfect match to satisfy their own inadequacies. However, they are also a perfect formula for a church which probably won't go anywhere. For, they have done all they wanted to do, by just getting together.

I don't know how I ever expected to make a living off of preaching, but when I arrived at Harvard Divinity School in 1975, being a pastor was not a live option. In fact, I prided myself and published the fact that I would never be a pastor. It was too much of a hassle. Then, one day during my first semester there, I was invited to preach at a vacant church in New Hampshire.

When I went to preach I had no inkling or idea of ever pastoring the church until after my sermon was over the chairman of the Deacon Board, who was also the chairman of the pulpit committee, said to me: "Reverend, a few of us have been talking and we like what we heard this morning. Do you mind if we included your name as a candidate for the pulpit?" Why did he have to do that?

This was the first time that any church had ever expressed an interest in me and frankly I was shocked, flattered, excited, nervous and scared all at once. What that deacon said to me touched a place in me which I did not know I had. I didn't take the time to talk to God. Of course, He would understand. So, I said immediately said: "No. Of course, not. I don't mind!"

As time progressed, whether I would be called, or not became of matter of whether I was better than the other preachers considered. Not whether I was better for the church or whether it was God's will. One of my buddies at the seminary was a leading candidate for the church also and now everyone knew that I was in the running. Pride took over and I was just as much concerned not to be embarrassed as I was to be called. In fact, if the whole thing could have taken place secretly, I probably would not have cared either way.

I remember driving through a blizzard on Christmas Day to preach in New Hampshire. I told my wife, the reason I was going was because I couldn't stand to see a church not have a preacher on Christmas Day, but really I just wanted one more chance to show that church how good of a pastor I would be.

When the vote was taken, my friend was called and I was not. I remember that my feeling was one of rejection and embarrassment. They wanted him, but they didn't want me. How could I now face my buddies and what would I say to my friend who had been called. In hindsight, I can see that my reaction in my disappointment proved my motives for wanting the church in the first place. It was all about my ego and my pride, not about my ministry and God's will. I vowed then, that I would never allow myself to be considered for a church again. I couldn't take the rejection. But it happened again.

I was minding my own business when I received a call to preach for a Youth Day at a church in Boston. I accepted the invitation and discovered that the church was vacant. I held my breath as I went. I told myself that I was not going to get caught up in this like I had in New Hampshire, but wouldn't you know it, after the service, the chairman of the pulpit committee came up to me and gave the same speech that the deacon had in New Hampshire, it was almost as if it were in a pulpit committee manual. He said: "You know, we don't have a pastor. Would you mind if we considered you as a candidate for the pulpit?" And before I could think, I said: "No, not at all!" There I was again.

This time, I thought I had the inside tract. Yet, this church didn't call me either. I don't know how true it was, but I heard that they didn't call me because I had too many children. They didn't believe that they could afford a pastor with a family, so they called a single man instead of me. *Whatever!*

Now, you know, by this time, I was devastated. I had been rejected twice within one year and each time, I just knew that I was the best candidate. Needless to say, I had learned my lesson and vowed to leave the pastorate alone. Well, it happened again!

This time, I had been invited to preach at a small congregational church in a small town called Brockton, Massachusetts, the home of boxer Marvin Hagler. I went. I preached and I was bitten again by the bug. (Doesn't anyone have a vaccine for this thing?) Anyway, my name was put into the hat again and once more, although the church vote was close (I got 15 and the other guy got 16!), I still was not called.

At this point I was too through. I was crushed. I was embarrassed. I was angry. I was really determined this time to leave pastoring alone and stop looking for a church. And finally I did. But you'll never guess what happened. As soon as I stopped looking, God started to working.

I was asked to preach at a Deacon's service in Providence, Rhode Island which is about an hour's drive from where we lived in Cambridge, Massachusetts. I went. I preached and, to this day, I don't know what I said, but whatever it was, the Lord blessed it.

After my sermon, there was a long line of people in front of me waiting to shake my hand and a man pushed his way passed all of them and said: "Hey, ya'll get out of the way. You have a pastor. We don't!" This man was the chairman of the pulpit committee of the largest church in that city. He got my name. I went back to preach at his church. At the age of twenty-three, they called me to be their pastor and the rest is history.

Not that size really makes all that difference, but for the record, I want you to see that the church which called me had a larger congregation than the combined total of the other three churches by which I had been rejected. Furthermore, the building of the church which called me was large enough to put the other three inside of and spin them around!

Here's the point. Stop trying to put yourself in a church and let God pick the place He wants you to serve. He's far better at it than you and I will ever be.

Do's and Don'ts to Deal With The Disease

To fight off the "I just gotta have a church" disease, try the following prescriptions:

1. ***Have confidence in and clarity about your call.*** Your basic foundation in ministry is to know without a doubt that the Lord has called you to preach. For if God has called you to preach, He will provide a place for you to preach.

2. ***Keep constant open communication with Christ.*** One great dangerous side effect of the "I've just gotta have a church bug" is that those who have it tend to stop listening to God and begin turning to everyone else for counsel. This is not the time to tune God out. It is the time to bend your knees, lift your eyes and open your ears to the voice of the Lord. He will speak. All you must do is listen.

3. ***Consider other areas of ministry.*** Being a pastor is not the only legitimate form of ministry. In fact, your personality, disposition and passion may equip you to serve elsewhere. Do what you have been designed and destined to do, not just what you desire to do.

4. ***Use the time you are looking for a church to prepare yourself so that when opportunity knocks you will be***

ready. In other words, don't just sit around twiddling your thumbs. Go to school. Take some continuing education classes. Sit under and learn from a great pastor. Teach in the church school. Visit nursing homes and prisons. Wait, yes! But, get busy and work in ministry until you are called.

5. ***Don't compare yourself, or your success with that of other preachers.*** They are not you and you are not them. When you compare yourself to other preachers, you usually end up with a false analysis because you seldom have all of the facts. You really don't know the price of their success, nor do you know what the Lord has in store for you. You may never be like the preacher across the street, but thank God that you don't have to be for God to tremendously bless you.

6. ***Never try to rationalize how churches chose their pastors.*** This will kill you. Most of the time, no matter how many PhD's, judges and lawyers a church may have on its pulpit committee, they rarely call a pastor based on what might be remotely called rational reasons. If you try to figure out church folk, you will go crazy, die and still never know why they act the way they do.

7. ***Just because you are not chosen by a church does not mean you have not been chosen by Him.*** Please

hear this. God has called you. God has chosen you. God has laid His hands on you. Don't seek security in the affirmation of the church. Rest your security and identity in the fact that He has called you out of darkness into the marvelous light.

8. ***You don't have to be the pastor of a church to begin pastoring people.*** Why are you sitting around waiting on some church to call you when there are millions of people who need ministry? Stop trying to get into a pulpit. Get busy. *Get into the ministry!* Remember Jesus never pastored a church, but what a great pastor he was! He discipled people. He healed people. He delivered people. He changed people. If you have His spirit in you and His call upon you, you can do the same as Jesus did, without a church.

9. ***Look for your status and fulfillment in Him not in a church.*** Whenever you get your status from a church, you are treading on thin ice. For, the church giveth and the church taketh away. Find your fulfillment and joy in knowing that you are a chosen and obedient servant of God.

10. ***Stop trying to get a church and ask God to give you a ministry.*** Have you ever stopped to think that the church God wants you to pastor may not exist yet. You and God may have to start it. In this case, you

must not wait for a church to call you. Instead, you must go forth and call a church!

I Know It Was the Blood... That Nearly Killed Me!

Third Sunday Communion was never complete in my hometown church until Deacon Luther Balis sang: "I know it was the blood that saved me!" He was a short dark skinned round man whose appearance did not match his gift. Deacon Balis was a chef by day. However, at prayer meetings, on weekends and especially third Sundays, he became a dignified baritone whose voice bellowed out down home hymns with a richness which could only be described as the Metropolitan Opera House being baptized in Mississippi.

Somewhere in every communion, during the days of his strength and the days of my youth, Deacon Balis would rise from his seat in the Senior Choir and raise his theme song. He would moan : "I know it was the blood! I know it was the blood. I know it was the blood that saved me. One day when I was lost, He died upon the cross, I know it was the blood that saved me!"

As a boy in Baltimore, Maryland, I learned the song "I know it was the blood that saved me!" from Deacon Balis, but when I became a man and began to serve as a pastor I found myself singing another song. It went like this: "I know it was the blood. I know it was the blood! I know it was the blood that *hung* me. Just when the vote was lost, I died upon the cross. I know it was the blood that *hung* me!"

It did not take me long to realize that churches tend to run according to blood and I do not mean the blood of Jesus. That is to say, more often than not, many of my proposals and programs died instant deaths because I had failed to understand that votes in the Baptist church very often follow family blood lines more than rational thought lines, or biblical guidelines.

The blessed ties that bound were family ties, friendship ties, fellowship ties and even foes' ties. The governing of a church was too often based on blood, not the Bible; relation not revelation; friendship not stewardship; and
common experience, not common sense.

Actually, I cannot complain. For in the more than twenty years that I have been a pastor, I have only lost a few church votes. But I can say that when I did lose a vote, virtually every time, it was the blood that hung me. One example will illustrate my point.

Several years ago, when I had only been at the church for two years, our church had a $250,000.00 renovation done to it. It added an elevator, a new chapel, a whole new floor and an elevated room which overlooked the sanctuary through an elegant glass wall. It was very nice.

Well, when we were preparing to dedicate the renovation, a reception was being planned which I thought would be good to have in the beautiful room overlooking the sanctuary. After all, the Governor of the State was going to be there, the city officials and, of course, all of our sincere and signifying members and friends. The caterers in our congregation agreed. They made ice carvings and just laid it out! It was a reception to end all receptions (and I mean that literally!).

Anyway, we had the reception and I thought all was well. Except for one minor detail. I had forgotten (or ignored) that the Board of Trustees had previously voted that there was to be no food ever served in that room. They said since it was on the third floor of the church, it would draw roaches upstairs and therefore have roaches all over the church.

At the Board meeting immediately after the reception they jumped all over me with both feet. "The Board voted that we would not have any food up there in that room and we want to know why you authorized the reception knowing that we had voted not to have food up there!" I was taken a back because I couldn't see the big deal. After all we were paying an exterminator. As far as I could see, just let him do his job.

I tried to explain that the room was perfect for that kind of thing. Why spend all of that money and not be able to use it. We went around for about three hours that night talking about *roaches*.

So, I decided to end the whole controversy by calling a special church business meeting to let the church decide if the Reverend was going to run the church or the roaches! What did I do that for? When the hour of the meeting came and I called the meeting to order, no sooner had I pronounced the phrase: "I am calling this special meeting to order," did I notice that the Trustees were sitting together in a body and the chairman of the Board of Trustees rose and said: "Brother moderator, I make a motion that we adjourn this meeting because it is an illegal meeting."

I could not believe my ears. I was furious. But I kept my cool. I then asked: "In what way?" He then proceeded to tell me that the pastor of the church could not call a special business meeting without having the church clerk get a petition from 50 members requesting the meeting and since that had not happened, the meeting was illegal.

I used to be a champion gymnast in my youth and I almost did a flip right there. I said: "Are you trying to tell me that as the pastor of this church, I do not have the right to call the church together and raise an issue?" His answer was: "Yes, not unless the clerk circulates a petition and gets the signature of fifty members requesting the meeting." I said: "I tell you what, we are going on with the meeting anyway." And we did. But I should have stopped it then, I might have made out better.

We went on and I told the church why the meeting had been called. We needed to settle the matter as to how the new room could be used. Could we have food functions up there or not. Once again, we went around for two or three hours, only this time it was the whole church. First, we discussed whether I had the right to call the meeting and then how eating upstairs would cause roaches to spread all over the building.

Finally, it came to a vote. I was confident that I would prevail because all of my people were there at the meeting. But to my surprise, when I saw one of the sainted mothers of the church stand and say: "Reverend, you know I love you , but if we eat upstairs, it really will cause more roaches!" I knew it was dead then. I was right because, the church voted not to eat up in that room.

When the vote did not go my way I turned to the chairman of the Board of Trustees and said publicly: "Now, if I were a different kind of person, I would nullify the vote based on the grounds that you said the meeting was illegal in the first place. However, the purpose of the meeting was to seek the will of the church and the church has spoken so that is that!"

Incidentally, at a subsequent meeting the church did vote specifically to give the pastor the right to call a special business meeting at any time as long as he gave the church two weeks notice and stated the purpose of the meeting. This power came back to help me and haunt me in the days to come. Nevertheless, I left that meeting defeated.

That night I began to analyze the defeat and wonder why my proposal did not pass. In the first place, it was a silly thing to call a special meeting for but you wouldn't know it because we were as serious as if we were discussing the proliferation of nuclear weapons. In the second place here we were supposedly educated, dignified and sophisticated people fussing about roaches. The third and perhaps most profound reason is that what to me was a meeting about roaches was really a meeting about power. Did what the trustees say go, or was it the pastor?

I had only been at the church about two years and had never tested whether the "Reverend we are with you's." on Sunday can translate into real votes at the business meeting on Monday. In retrospect, I realized that when the people stood to vote that night I saw people whom I had never seen before. They were brothers, sisters, uncles, aunts, first cousins, second cousins, third cousins, long lost sons and daughters, war buddies, and even ex- spouses of the church officers. The numbers of these were large enough to make the difference. Many of these people never came to church with any regularity, if at all. However, they were able to capitalize on our poor membership record keeping to show up and show this young boy not to mess with *their* momma and daddy.

Before then and since then, I have seen business meetings swayed by signals passed between kin folk. I have seen votes passed or failed based on the nay saying of one patriarch. I've witnessed voting blocks formed based on being in the same family, hailing from the same state, graduating from the same school, belonging to the same sorority, or fraternity, being members of the same

Masonic lodge, being set free from the same plantation, or shouting on the same foot!

The reason that I am bringing this all of this up is because those preachers who do not know, need to know that unfortunately in our churches, it may not be enough to be right to win a church vote. I am not suggesting that pastors stoop to party politics in the house of God. However, I am saying that they need to understand that the dynamic which runs many churches is the blood that runs in the members veins, *not* the blood that flows from Calvary's mountain.

You Can't Be Serious!

Not that most pastors need any help, but if you really want to get yourself into deep trouble and stay there, I dare you to be serious! Many churches are rather tolerant of their pastors in certain areas. It is okay for them to be sophisticated. In fact, they like that. It is fine for their pastor to be a little sanctimonious. That's okay too. After all he is a preacher and should be a little holier than thou, right? We don't really say it out loud, but it is even acceptable and almost desirable that the pastor is even sexy! However, no matter how sophisticated, sanctimonious, or sexy he, or she may be. The line is drawn when the pastor gets to be too serious.

By serious, I do not mean walking around with a long face or having a morbid demeanor. What I mean is that the pastor is not playing church and will not accept anything less than what the gospel requires from the church. Many churches operate on the level of the superficial and have for so long that when they are challenged to be serious about the gospel they preach and teach, whoever is doing the challenging is writing their own ticket out of the door!

It is sad to say, but too many churches are more serious about their name than His name. Too many choirs are more serious about their robes than His praise. Too many deacons are more serious about their front row seats than His top priority in their lives. Too many trustees are more serious about counting money than giving money. Too many ushers are more serious about prancing around the church, than standing up for Him. And yes, too many preachers are more serious about the size of their membership than the level of their congregation's discipleship.

You are too serious when you demand that deacons attend prayer meeting. You are too serious when you don't allow anybody to count the tithes who does not pay tithes. You are too serious when you expect church school teachers to themselves be taught. You are too serious when you let homeless people into your stain glassed hideout. You are too serious when you try to do it just like Jesus did. You are too serious when you look for miracles. You are too serious when you think that people will actually stay in church more than two hours and then come back for an afternoon service.

We have been getting way with spiritual murder for years and whenever anyone, preacher or otherwise, starts to get too serious, the church has a problem. One reaction is *not* to take the pastor seriously when he or she gets serious. Another response is for the church to be as serious about maintaining mayhem as the pastor is about establishing order. A third tactic would be to paint the pastor as a lunatic for expecting Christians to actually follow the Bible and practice what they preach.

As I recall, just about every time I got into trouble during my years of pastoring was at the point when I decided to get serious. Can you stand an example?

Once in my early years of pastoring, our church appointed a man to the trustee board. He seemed to be a fine enough fellow. He had a pretty good business head on his shoulders. Compared to several of the other members on the board he was fairly young. He seemed to be a welcomed addition to the church's leadership.

But, when he was nominated and elected to the trustee board, everyone in the church, except me, knew that he was living out of wedlock with one of the deacon's sister-in-law. Since I didn't know it, of course, it didn't bother me until we had a deacon's retreat and the matter came up.

Each deacon to a man, including the deacon whose sister in law was involved, adamantly chimed in that something should be done about that. No self respecting church should have a trustee on the board who was shacking up right out in the open. If the pastor was a man and the deacons were men, they would do something about it. We vowed that we would.

Apparently, some other members were upset too because I remember passing an eighty year old member on the stairs one day and as we passed she said: “Now Reverend, you know that ain't right.” I said: “What ain't right?” She said: “You know, having that man on the Trustee Board and all the time he's living with a woman that's not his wife. Somebody ought to do something.” I assured her that the deacons and I had already talked about it and were planning to take care of the matter.

When the time for the annual meeting came, I noticed before the meeting that the man's name had been renominated by the nominating committee to serve another term as a trustee. So, in an effort to avoid a public confrontation, I called the brother and told him that we appreciated his service and knew he had much to offer, but that it did not send the right message to the church, the community or to Christ to have a leader of the church living in such an arrangement. I told him that if his name did in fact come up during the meeting that I would rise to oppose his nomination.

At first, there was silence and then he said: “Okay. I understand.” I wiped the sweat from my brow and began to get ready for the meeting that night. Then, just as I was about to leave the house, the phone rang. It was the trustee. He said at first he wasn't going to fight it, but he had just gotten off of the phone with his mother down south and she told him since he was as good as anybody else in the church, he should not bow out. Of course, he listened to his mother over his pastor!

I had hoped to avoid a scene, but if we had to vote on the issue, I knew there would be no problem because I knew that the deacons were 100% behind it and the whole church was talking about it. When the names to be nominated for trustees were read, I rose from my seat (I was not the moderator of the church!) and said: "Brother moderator, I would like for the church to vote tonight to exclude the name of brother so and so from the list of persons to serve as trustees." Then, the moderator who was a deacon who had been at the retreat and was also the brother in law of the woman living with the trustee turned to me and asked: "On what grounds?"

Now, I was really in trouble. I did not think it proper to expose this brother's situation even though I thought most of the people in the room knew what was up. If I told the problem, then I thought that the people's confidence in my confidentiality would be damaged. So I said: "Brother moderator, I would rather not share the reason, but as your pastor I would hope that you would trust me and know that there is a reason and leave it at that." Then from the back somebody shouted: "Tell us! Tell us! What did he do?" I stood my ground and only repeated that they should trust me on this one.

We went round and round for a while and then it finally came to a vote. There were 109 people in the room and the vote was 12 to 9 to keep him on the board! Mind you I had 13 deacons which meant that if all of them had voted like they said they were going to, it would have passed. But not only did the deacons not all vote against keeping him on the board, half of the deacons voted to keep him on the board. And the rest of the ninety some people just took the fifth amendment. So, there I was in front of the whole church all by myself because I was too serious.

After the meeting, the eighty year old member who had earlier complained that it wasn't right said: "Now you know Reverend, if you take him off, you would have to take the rest of them off too!" The deacons who voted to keep him on the board said that they did it because they had time to think about it (which means they went home and talked to their wives) and they felt if they got rid of him, then so many other people in the church with *personal problems* might lose their positions. Where would the line be drawn?

Think for a moment what would have to change in our churches and in us if we were really serious about being disciples of Christ. If we were serious about our worship and praise to God would the same people be leading it? If we were serious about our leadership would the same people be in it? If we were serious about mission would it be relegated to the fifth Sunday afternoon? If we were serious about evangelism would it be the responsibility of just two or three members on the evangelism committee? If we were serious about prayer would people have to be begged to come to prayer meeting? If we were serious about praise would we have to be pumped up all the time in order to give Him praise? If we were serious about excellence would we accept mediocrity?

I think both you and I know that the pastor who takes the gospel too seriously is in for it from his own people no matter how diplomatically he does it. This puts the pastor in a catch 22. For, if he is serious, he gets it from the people. But if he is not serious he will get it from God. So I ask you what I have constantly had to ask myself: *"To whom would you rather answer, mortal people who refuse to do right or an almighty God would refuses to accept wrong?"*

Waiting on Folk to Die

It was about ten, or eleven o'clock on the Saturday night before a much publicized and politicized church business meeting when my telephone rang. After I picked up the phone, I heard the voice of a preacher who was calling me from almost two thousand miles away on the west coast. This preacher was an acquaintance of mine whom I did not really know knew I existed. He was a very visible and respected leader in one of the national Baptist conventions. I was surprised that he cared enough to call and surprised at what he had to say.

He said: "Dexter this is ----. I've been hearing about the trouble you've been having there over the past few months and I'm calling you as a friend to offer you some unsolicited advice. I know that it is none of my business and if you want to you can tell me its none of my damn business and hang up the phone, but I just wanted to call to encourage you."

Well, I did not know how to respond to an intro like that. On the one hand I did need some advice and encouragement, but on the other hand anytime somebody begins by saying you could tell me it's none of my damn business, then they are probably right. However, I took a chance and just listened.

He continued by saying I heard that you had a vote a few weeks ago to choose some land and that it was very close. I said: "Yes. That's right." "Well," he said, "I think that you should just drop the whole thing because the church is divided and there is no way that even if you win the vote that you can get the job done. You should do what I did. If they do not want to move, just buy up property around the church and add on. Give them what they want. Then, you get you a hobby and to hell with them Niggers. If they want to go forward let them, if not let them stand still, but you find you something that fulfills you and don't worry about it. The church will probably split anyway. Just forget it. It is not worth it!"

Then, he laid this line on me. He said: "Besides, you are only 35 years old and the people that are giving you so much hell are twice your age. All you need to do is preach the gospel and just wait for a few of those hellions to die and in 10 to 15 years, you'll be the pastor of the church and won't have the headache you are having now."

The advice continued along this vain for several more minutes and then it ended when he asked: "Well, what are you going to do?" I said: "We are going to have the meeting and we are going to vote, but thanks for calling! I'll let you know how the vote turns out."

There is no doubt in my mind that this preacher was genuinely concerned about me and believed that he was saving me some trouble by telling me to forget it and just wait for the old hellions to die. However, although he was not the first one to suggest this to me, his advice was hard to take.

The whole notion of pastoring a church waiting with baited breath for the phone call which tells you that your arch enemy in the church has just been run over by a Mack truck on the way to file papers to sue you again is not only unchristian, but it just does not make common sense.

Here we are supposed to be bringing new life and at the same time waiting on folk to die; pre-preaching their funerals; asking them how they are doing and hoping they are near 'bout dead; looking in the obituaries each day for to make your day by seeing the name of someone who's a thorn in your side; checking the sick list each week hoping to see the name of someone you love to hate; going to visit them in the hospital and not praying for healing but that The Lord's will be done!; and doing like they say morticians do, sizing up the living for caskets.

If you are a preacher or pastor waiting for someone else to die so that you can be free to do God's will, consider the following:

1. ***Why should you put your life on hold waiting for other people to die?*** This is surely no way for *you* to live.

2. ***Just because certain individuals die does not take away a certain mean spirit in a church.*** What is wrong with many of our churches is much bigger than any one individual. It would take a major plague and several decades to get rid of all of the hellions in some churches. Besides, there are times when a contrary spirit has possessed a church. This spirit cannot be simply carried out in the casket of one or two people. It must be cast out by the Holy Spirit of God.

3. ***People train their children to take their place.*** At the death of your arch enemy you will learn that along the way he has trained several disciples in the church to take his place. Furthermore, at the funeral, his wayward child who hasn't been to church in twenty years, will suddenly get religion and vow over his daddy's open casket: "Don't worry Dad, I'll be here to

carry on the fight!" Believe me, junior is often ten times the troublemaker that his daddy was.

4. ***Other people join the church who are worse.*** You think that you have identified the people you would like to die and they actually do die. Then, you open the doors of the church one Sunday and in walk several new members who were put out of the church down the street. You are their next victim. Are you now going to start a new death list?

5. ***It presupposes that God cannot work in spite of opposition.*** Waiting on folk to die indicates that you believe the only way for God to have the victory is for Him to strike someone dead. Sometimes, God gets the victory by keeping them alive and preparing a table before you in their presence. Jesus fled Bethlehem and went to Egypt and waited for Herod to die. However, Joseph was told to do it in a dream and at the time Jesus was a new born baby. Notice though that when He was a full grown man in Gethsemene and His hour had come, He did not ask for Pilate or Judas to die. He simply said: "Father not my will but thine be done." He faced the cross and rose on the third day while Pilate still lived.

6. ***You will die inside while waiting on others to die.*** Waiting on them to die will kill you. The people in the wilderness had to die out before a new generation could go into the promised land, but don't ever forget that Moses had to die with them too! Do you want to be like Moses and die in the wilderness with a bunch of hard headed people or do you want to be like Joshua and cross over the Jordan with a caring, courageous and visionary new generation?

7. ***Even if they get sick, they never seem to die.*** Why is it that the wrong people die. I know God knows what He is doing, but when you start waiting for people to die. The ones you depend on and rely on die first and the others, like duracell batteries, just keep going and going and going! Fighting the pastor gives some people a new lease on life and a reason for living. I had a trustee once who had a heart attack and went to the hospital. I went to see him and he told me that when he came back to church, I was going to see a completely different man. I thought he meant he was going to straighten up. Not a chance. He got worse! The good seem to die young and the rest live forever, getting more devious with age.

8. ***You cannot pastor people who have not yet joined your church.*** You must serve those who already belong, or else the new members you expect to attract

will never come. Waiting on folk to die not only puts your life on hold, but it also puts your entire church's ministry on hold. It is impossible to wait on certain people to die without killing whatever other ministry there may still be left in the church. Focus on that which yet lives. Revive, or if necessary, resurrect it.

There is something radically wrong when you are in a church and the only way you see out of your dilemma is to wait until somebody dies. For, it is not very far from thinking: "I hope they hurry up and die." to "Why can't I help them die?"

God did not call preachers or parishioners to be at each other's throats. There are too many souls to be won for the church to be spending any of its time praying for the death of the saints.

What can you do instead of homicide or suicide?

1. ***Share the vision with a few who are ready to receive it.*** Work closely with this group. Even if they are not currently leaders in the church. Disciple this group. Then, pray that the vision will break out in the rest of the church.

2. ***Create another vehicle to make the dream come alive.*** There is more than one way to skin a cat. Maybe what you want to do can be done more effectively through the creation of a non-profit corporation. Such a corporation could easily be structured so that great things could be done by a few people with virtually no red tape.

3. ***Wait on the vision to live, not for people to die.*** There is a difference! Instead of looking to see live people in caskets. Seek to see new life from dry bones. Remember:

> *"Write the vision, and make it plain upon tablets, that he may run that readeth it. For the vision is yet for an appointed time, but at the end it shall speak, and not lie: though it tarry, wait for it; because it will surely come, it will not tarry." (Habakkuk 2:2-3)*

If It Weren't for My Wife

There is something to be said for being single, especially when it comes to ministry. I must agree with both Jesus and Paul that if a person wants to go into the ministry and can bear living without sexual intimacy, they might be better off single. As Paul suggests, when a person is married, they must seek to please their spouse. However, when they are single, they are more free to please and serve the Lord.

Now, having said that, I come to the fact that many if not most ministers are married. Some were ministers when they got married. Others became ministers after they had already been married. For many ministers, men in particular, being married has been a major source of problems to their ministry.

My wife was the one who wrote the book: *Sick and Tired of Being a Minister's Wife*, but I must confess to you that while she was going through her ordeal, she was not the only one who was sick and tired. In fact, I have often wondered what my life would have been like if it weren't for my wife.

If it weren't for my wife, I would have had more peace in the church. Why couldn't I have married a meek and mild woman who would just sit still and be quiet on the second row like all the other ministers' wives? Not my wife!

I shall never forget how she was elected by the women of the church to be the chairperson of Women's Day for a given year. That seemed innocent enough. In fact, it demonstrated their love and respect for her. That is, until she had a brilliant idea. She wanted to change the color of dresses that the women wore on Woman's Day.

For more than fifty years the woman of the church wore all white on their day. This year, however, my wife suggested that they all wear yellow. At the meeting where the decision was made, the women agreed. But after the meeting, some of them fussed and fussed and then fussed some more. I wondered, how in the world could so much controversy be raised over a color?

It got so bad, that I said to my wife: "Well, why don't you just leave it like it was or maybe just use yellow as the accent color. Then, those who wanted to, could still wear white." What did I have to say that for! Now, I was one of them. So, I left it alone.

On Woman's Day, some women came dressed in yellow, some came in yellow and white, some came in all white and some just plain didn't come. Actually, it turned out fine, but not without my blood pressure going on a roller coaster ride.

If it weren't for my wife, I could have gone farther in my career. After many years of preaching I had become in demand. I was being asked to speak all over the country for virtually any and every occasion. This included revivals where I would have to be away from home for several consecutive days.

As I saw it, this was what I had been called to do. And I loved it, going to different towns, preaching at "major houses", lecturing at leading colleges, meeting the movers and shakers of our denomination. It was great. These were all necessary steps to building a name and reputation as one of God's "bad boys."

For my wife, though, all of this was a great burden. I am sure that she didn't mind me being "successful," but she did mind having to handle four little children by herself while I was away preaching like a fool and being treated like a king.

In her own way, she impressed this fact upon me, time and time again. So, I cut back my preaching out of town and literally did not accept certain engagements because it would have caused me to be away too much. Many times, I have wondered, what if I could have just gone and gone and gone?

If it weren't for my wife, I wouldn't be under so much pressure to produce finances. My wife likes nice things, but when our children were young, she refused to work outside of the home. Mind you, my wife has a Master's degree from Johns Hopkins University.

My thinking was that since she liked nice things, she could have gotten a part time job. Help a brother out! Do something. Do anything! But no, she wanted to stay home and raise our children herself. Believe me, in the long run, that was the right choice, but at the time it seemed like all of the financial weight was on me.

If it weren't for my wife, I wouldn't be tied down to mundane things. I know that Monday is trash day, so why does my wife have to announce first thing every Monday: "Don't forget today is trash day." Why must she regularly remind me of the mundane stuff! Cut the grass! Wash the car! Rake the leaves! Go to the grocery store! Pick up your clothes! Straighten up your office! Clean out the garage!

Doesn't she know that I am the pastor of a big church? Isn't she aware that I need to be free to fellowship with the Father? I've got to be available to the Lord. At anytime revelation might break in.

The reason why this chapter is in the section entitled "Traps of Typical Preachers" is because your marriage can be one, if you are not careful. I know that the things I have mentioned above are the sentiments of many preachers. However, Satan will trick you and then trap you. He will make you believe that the very one who God placed beside you to help you, is your greatest hindrance.

In the early days of my ministry and my marriage, sometimes I saw my wife as a burden that I had to bear, instead of a blessing which I could enjoy. Now, after four children, three churches, twenty-five years of marriage, *and her enlightenment*, I have come to see her and love her in a different and deeper way. I can see that what she had been trying to do for me all along was simply help me.

Today, if you asked me to fill in the blank: "If it weren't for my wife______.", here's what I would say:

If it weren't for my wife, I would have no protection from other women. The fact that I have a wife keeps some women away. The fact that I pubicly express my love for my wife, keeps others away. The fact that my wife satisfies me in every way, keeps me away from other women! In a real sense, she is my covering when it comes to other women. She protects me from them. They don't bother me because they don't want to deal with her.

If it weren't for my wife, I may not see the evil side of other people. It is not that I am naive. It is only that I look for the good in people and often over look the evil in them. Ninety-nine per cent of the time my wife is able to pick up on and discern traits about people which I completely miss. Ninety-nine per cent of the time I ignore her and ninety nine per cent of the time she is right. In my old age, I am learning to rely on *her* gifts of discernment as one of God's gifts to *me*.

If it weren't for my wife, I wouldn't have any nice things. I told you that my wife likes nice things. She is not extravagant, but she does like nice things. She is the kind of person who goes into a store and is immediately attracted to the most expensive thing in the store and will settle for nothing less. Now, if it were left up to me, just give me a bible, a microphone and a crowd and I'm set! Not so with my wife.

The up side of this is that if it were not for her insistence, I probably would not live in the house I live in, drive the car I drive, wear the clothes I wear or enjoy the life I do. When it comes to certain necessary and needful things, I don't care, but thank God she does.

If it weren't for my wife, I wouldn't be so humble. It never seems to fail. Just when I feel like I am all of that and a bag of chips, here comes my wife to remind me of who I am and what I am not. It never feels good when someone dear to you bursts your inflated ego, but it is always good for you when you have someone who will. It is far better to have someone who loves you to do it than your enemy. Your wife is trying to assist you. Your enemy is trying to assassinate you.

Whenever I even attempt to get puffed up, all I have to do think about my wife. She can get me straight because next to God, nobody knows the real me any better.

If it weren't for my wife, I would have no one to minister to me. My wife is my minister. She doesn't preach to me. She doesn't read me scripture. But she does counsel me. She comforts me. She prays for me. She cheers for me. She affirms me. She encourages me. She supports me. She defends me. She loves me. If she did not do the things she does for me at home, I would not be able to do the things I do for the people at church and in the community.

If it weren't for my wife, I might never hear the truth. People of power are surrounded by a host of groupies who don't always tell the truth. To them you are smarter than you really are. They say you are a better preacher than you really are. They tell you that you are better looking than you really are. They tell you that you are not in as much trouble as you really are. A good wife, like mine, does not lie to you. She tells you the truth even if it takes you a few days to talk to her afterwards.

If it weren't for my wife, I would not have a best friend. It is said that man's best friend is his dog. Yet, I am convinced that a male preacher's best friend is and should be his wife. You can trust her when you cannot trust anyone else. You can tell her your heart's secrets when you dare not reveal them to anyone else. You can be yourself around her without fear of rejection.

If it weren't for my wife, I might not be free. All of the gifts that my wife bring to me add up to freedom. I am free from scandal because I am protected from other women. I am free from deceitful ones because I have the advantage of her sensitivities. I am free from pride because she keeps me humble. I am free from shabbiness because she makes me buy nice things. I am free from self-delusion because she tells me the truth. I am free from loneliness because she is my best friend. I am free to be me, because she loves me no matter what!

My brother, if you are struggling in your marriage and your ministry because you think your wife gets in the way, don't forget this. The woman you married, the woman whom you love is not your enemy. She is your greatest asset. She is not a thorn in your side. She is the mighty wind beneath your wings. Love her. Cherish her. Take care of her. Minister to her. For, when the chips are down, and friends get few, all you may have left is her!

Trying to Fight the Lord's Battles

Samuel was a prophet and judge who ruled Israel. He led his people through a time of turmoil to a time of peace and prosperity. One day a great crisis arose when the people of Israel demanded that he appoint them a king.

The Israelites looked around at other nations. These nations had kings, so Israel wanted one too. Samuel tried to tell them that God was their king; they did not need to have a king; and if they did get a king, he would tax their property and send their sons off to war. Nevertheless, Israel would not hear him. They wanted a king.

In frustration, Samuel took the matter to God. Much to his surprise, God told Samuel, in effect, "Don't let it bother you because they have not rejected you, they have rejected me. If they want a king, let them have one."

Now Samuel was angry with God because He seemed to care more about God's honor than God did. The prophet's problem was that he was trying to fight the Lord's battle. At the Red Sea, God told Moses stand still, see the salvation of the Lord ... the Lord will fight for you. In this case, Samuel was trying to fight for the Lord.

Trying to fight the Lord's battle is a major temptation for prophets because:

1. ***They think, just because they are in the fight that it is their fight.*** What we fail to realize as we stand up for God is that these issues that we face are an extension of an age old conflict between God and the forces of darkness. Satan is not mad at us. He is mad at God. But since he can't get to God, he gets to us. One thing we must always remember is that we are called to fight, but it is not our fight. It's the Lord's.

2. ***They think, just because they know what to do, that what they want to do is what God wants to be done!*** We are like the disciples whose first reaction to opposition is to call down fire from on high. Yet, this is not always the approach that the Lord wants. No matter how long we have been in the ministry, we must not only remember that the fight is not ours, but also that the way it is to be fought is not up to us.

3. ***They think, just because they are in leadership that they are responsible for how it ends up.*** For me, this is the greatest problem. For, I am the one out in front. I am the one seen leading the charge. I am the one who

will be talked about if this fight ends up a flop. I have my integrity on the line. I have to make sure we win. There's too much at stake. Here again, we err. What's at stake is not your reputation, but God's. Make no mistake about it, God knows how to defend Himself. Stop seeing the battle you are in as being all about you. Know that if you are fighting for what is right, it is really all about Him.

4. ***They think they know all of the factors and players.*** There is no way for any prophet to know all of the players, or factors in one of God's fights. How could Moses have known that the wind was going to help them at the Red Sea? How could the three Hebrew boys have known that the Son of God was going to join them in the firery furnace? How was the widow to have known that the Lord was going to multiply her meal? We never know what else needs to be factored into one of God's fights as a another potential foe, or an unexpected vehicle to victory.

While trying to fight the Lord's battle is a major temptation for prophets, it is a major temptation which prophets should resist because:

1. ***God has His own when (time).*** Timing is everything and no one has better timing than God. Our time is not God's time. When we say: "Enough!", God says:

"You've got some more to go!" We say: "Now!" and God says: "Not, yet!" The old saints have always sung and said: "You can't hurry God. No. You've just got to wait. You've got to trust Him and give Him time. No matter how long it takes. He's a God that you can't hurry. He'll be there don't you worry. He may not come when you want Him, but He's always right on time."

2. ***God has His own way.*** Who would ever think that God would solve the matter of human sin, by sending His own son to die. This is not rational. This is not normal. For sure, this was not expected. It is safe to say it is not the way I would have handled the situation! However, God's ways are not our ways. Indeed, His ways are past finding out. Nevertheless, His sometimes inscrutible way is the best to face and fight a foe.

3. ***God has His own weapons.*** Our weapon of choice may be the tongue, or the gun. Both of these come in handy for a quick (but not necessarily permanent) resolution of conflict. Yet, God has been known to use some strange weapons to fight with. David killed Goliath with a sling shot. Samson slew one thousand Philistines with the jawbone of an ass. Joshua beat the Amalekites with the uplifted hands of Moses. God has to fight His way and use His own weapons.

4. ***God has His own warriors.*** Most of the time, none of us would pick the same people to be on our side that God does. If I were Jesus, I would never have picked the disciples He did. If I were Hosea, I never would have married the wife he did. If I were God, I never would have used Saul of Tarsus like He did. God is the coach of His team. He reserves the right to pick the players and send them in and bring others out according to His will.

Once we have settled the fact that the battle is the Lord's and not ours, how do we handle a fight? We are certainly going to be involved in them. Here's what you do.

1. ***Pray about it.*** Before you tackle it and before you enter it, pray about it. Ask God to show you the real issue. Ask God to show you the real players. Ask God to show you your real strength. Ask God to show you how to fight it.

2. ***Present it.*** By this I mean, make public the issue which may result in a fight. This could be something as simple as adding drums to your Sunday worship or as major as building a new church. Either way, after you have prayed about it, don't keep it to yourself, present it. You may choose a smaller audience at first, but by all means, present it.

3. ***Pursue it.*** If the initial response to your proposal is not altogether enthusiastic, don't give up right away. Pursue it. Meet with every necessary committee. Turn over every necessary stone. Do what you have to do. Give it your best shot. You believe this thing to be of God, so go all out.

4. ***Have a peace about it.*** Suppose you have prayed about it, you have presented, you have pursued it and still have nothing to show for it? My advice in this case is to keep on pursuing it until God gives you a peace about it. He will either give you a peace that what you are seeking will come to pass later or give you permission to drop it completely. *The important point is that if God has called you to a task, you must give it all you've got until He gives you a peace about it.*

Obedience Is Better Than Sacrifice...
And Cheaper Too!

In I Samuel 15, the prophet of the Lord, Samuel is sent by God to anoint Saul the king of Israel and to instruct him to make war against the Amalekites. God's command to Saul through Samuel was to go against the Amalekites and utterly destroy them and all that they had because they warred against Israel when they left Egypt.

Saul promptly accepted the anointing and the assignment. He assembled together an army of 200,000 footmen and 10,000 men of Judah. This army laid in wait outside of the land of the Amalekites. Finally, Israel under the leadership of king Saul, attacked. And attack they did. With seemingly no trouble at all, they chased and wiped out the Amalekites over a long distance, but in very short order.

Now, the command of the Lord to Saul was to utterly destroy everything that the Amalekites had, but he and his people had a better idea. They thought it would be a waste to destroy the good things which they discovered in the land of the Amalekites. Besides that, they could sacrifice the goats, sheep and oxen to the Lord. They were sure God would be pleased. Therefore, they destroyed everything that was worthless and brought everything of value back with them to their camp, including Agag, the king of the Amalekites.

In the night, the Lord told Samuel what Saul had done and that He was sorry that He had ever made Saul king in the first place. This news grieved Samuel because he remembered how he had protested Israel having any king other than God when the people first asked him to anoint them a king (I Samuel 8). Now, after the sin of Saul, it was Samuel's lot to tell Saul that because he (Saul) had rejected God, that God had rejected him from being king of Israel.

When Samuel confronted Saul with his disobedience, Saul protested that he did obey the Lord. He destroyed the Amalekites as the Lord had said. He thought that he was doing God a favor by bringing back the spoils as a sign of victory and as an offering of sacrifice. When Samuel responded that this was not the exact command of the Lord, Saul shifted the blame and said that it was not his fault, but the fault of the people. In the end when pressed by Samuel, he was forced to admit that it was his own fault, but because he feared the people he allowed them to disobey the command of the Lord with his tacit and passive permission.

It is during this exchange between Samuel and Saul over his disobedience that we read those fateful words: "Hath the Lord as great delight in burnt offerings and sacrifice, as in obeying the voice of the Lord? Behold, to obey is better than sacrifice and to hearken than the fat of rams." (I Samuel 15:22)

As a result of his sin, Saul was irrevocably rejected from being king of Israel even though he continued to sit on the throne. He found out that day that obedience is not only better than sacrifice, but cheaper too. *The price of obedience is a bargain compared to the costs of disobeying what we know to be the will of God.*

Unforntuately, before and since Saul, people of God have had to learn this lesson over and over again. I too had to learn it and pay a high price for the knowledge of it. Let me tell you how.

I knew from the first day I saw our church that it was too small for the vision God had given me for it. This may sound amazing when one considers the fact that it was three stories high, seated more than 1000 people, had excellent parking compared to church parking in most large cities. It was centrally located. It was a monument and testament to the determination of a pastor and people who built it and the God whose grace allowed it.

Nevertheless, it took me seven years of being pastor there to muster enough courage to utter that thought to anyone other than my wife. Yet, I had known it all the time. I knew how much many of the people loved their building and were proud of their history on that spot.

Still, quite frankly, I was not prepared to tackle the issue of building a new church on another site because I felt that I would then be tackled from all sides. So I kept putting it off.

Finally, after we had gone to two services, jammed and overflowed our parking lots, and were called upon to do some substantial repair to the 70 year old building, it was clear to me that now was the time to take the bull by the horns and tell the people what the Lord had shown me.

I shall never forget. This realization and determination came to me while I was on vacation one August. I remember that was the summer I began to grow a beard with the vow that I would not shave it off until we built our new church. When I returned from my vacation, beard and all, I ran into one of our church's most influential members and one of my most trusted friends. He was an old deacon in his eighties who had no formal education, but who was one of the wisest men I have ever known, especially in the area of "churchianity."

We sat on the front steps of the church that afternoon and I told him what the Lord had told me. He did not leap for joy and shout up and down the street, but he took it quite well. In fact, I could see in his eyes that he saw what would be in store for both me as an individual and the church as an institution. Still, he encouraged me to do what the Lord had put in my mind. As far as he was concerned, he helped pay for that 70 year old building and he would help build the next one.

From his response I was encouraged to move ahead and I did. I called a meeting of the church officers and leaders which was held at a local hotel. There, I told them of the vision to build a new church on a new site. And asked their agreement to secure the services of a professional Capital Fund raiser to help us raise the necessary funds to build because what I had in mind was going to cost in the millions.

To my surprise, there were a few questions, but nothing I regarded as serious or negative. When I called for a show of support for the idea, virtually everyone stood! And if there was anyone in the room that day who was against the idea, they did not stand or voice their opposition.

Boy, I was on a roll! So next, I called the entire church together. The members were asked to stay back after worship one Sunday morning and I shared the vision with them. When I laid out reasons why something had to be done about our future and then concluded that the only rational and right thing to do was to build a new church on another site. The people stood, clapped and applauded. They were so excited that I said to myself. You dummy, the people have known this a long time and they have just been waiting for someone who had the courage to lead them where they always knew they would someday have to go!

That Sunday the church accepted the plan to build a new church on another site by an overwhelming majority and authorized me to appoint a committee to search the city for a tract of land which would be suitable for our expanded vision and continual growth. This I did and we were off and running.

After six or seven months of research, our blue ribbon panel on the land search came back with at least ten possible and available pieces of land. At the top of the list were two pieces of land. Second was a 34 acre pretty piece of flat land with a lot of trees. The at the top of the list was a 30 acre site which sat on top of a hill. It had three ponds on it. Had several lower acres which were bordered by a creek and it was surrounded by a one hundred acre golf course. Our second choice was more land, but it was not as diverse and scenic as the first choice. Besides, we could never get in touch with the owners of the second property.

We settled on the thirty acre site by the golf course because of its beauty and because, the theme for our ministry from day one had been "A city set on a hill, making disciples for Christ." This land was on a hill!

After the committee and I had agreed that this was the land for us, I asked the Chairman of our Deacon Board and the chairman of our Trustee Board to meet me out there one day. We walked the grounds and saw endless possibilities together.

Then, we did something which shall forever prove pivotal. We went over and stood under a large tree on the land. We joined hands and prayed. That afternoon we asked the Lord to give us that land by the golf course so that we could do His will and build a city set on a hill which would make disciples for Jesus Christ. When the prayer had ended, I was convinced that it had already been answered.

I called a church meeting and the committee presented their recommendation to the church. By then, the opposition had begun to mount especially when it was obvious that we were actually going to do this. At that meeting about the land, several people protested that they had not had a chance to personally look at and study the land.

As far as I was concerned, that was the committee's job. They had done their job. So let's vote on the matter one way or the other. The church voted to accept the recommendation of the committee and pursue getting a contract on the land for the purpose of building a new church there. The margin of victory was less than the margin which initially approved the project, but it was a clear majority.

We interpreted that church vote as another go sign and went into negotiations on the 30 acre site by the golf course. We asked the owner to send us a contract and he did. The asking price was $300,000.00 which was no real problem. However, there was a clause in the contract which said that before the owner would sell to us, we would have to agree not to build anything on that site other than a church without his written permission. That is, even after we owned it. Then, we would have to approve of the sale of alcohol in the club house of his golf course across the street.

I thought he was nuts. If he thought we were going to pay $300,000.00 for a piece of property and then have to ask his permission before we could do anything on it, he was crazy. Then, to ask a church pastored by the original “I Ain't Into That!” Rapping Reverend to publicly and in writing approve of the sale of alcohol across the street from the church was impossible. The leaders of our church talked about these issues and decided right away we had better look for another piece of land. *Remember this is the land we prayed and asked the Lord to give us.*

While we were looking, from out of the blue I got a call from California and it was one of the owners of the 34 acre site which had been our second choice. He had somehow finally heard about our need for land and was willing to sell it to us. Wow! I thought. You see how God works. One door closes and another opens! (But I had never asked God for *this* land!)

The owners and the leaders of our church got together. The asking price was $275,000.00 and we decided to jump on it. After all, it was 4 more acres than the other site. It was $25,000.00 cheaper and it came with no strings attached! This must be it, we thought. We secured a contract on the second site, took it to the church and by a narrow margin voted to buy this site instead of the first one!

Earnest money was put down, a closing date was set and we were on our way, so we thought. However, while our lawyers were doing their due diligence on the closing process they discovered that a zoning change would be required in order for a church to be built on that site. The lawyers did not seem to think that the zoning change would be denied. They only wanted us to know that it would cost more money and create a delay. Within days of this disclosure of our attorneys, somehow the word about the zoning had either leaked out or was figured out, by the opposition and the next thing we knew, we were hit with a restraining order from a judge to keep us from buying the land.

We had sense enough to know not to buy land that we could not use. That was why we didn't get the first piece of land. However, the members in our church who were against building and moving didn't think we had that much sense. They were looking for a way to stop us and they had finally found it. *This is how we got into court - trying to buy a piece of land that we had not prayed over.*

From this point on, things got progressively worse and everything I did whether related to building a new church, or not was simply added on to the plaintiffs compliant and we were back in court again and again. Eventually, the date of the offer on the second piece of land expired and buying the land had become a moot point because the contract had expired.

By then, the land was the furthest thing from my mind. I was literally fighting for my safety and sanity in the church. We had court suits flying everywhere. Our church meetings were like the World Wrestling Federation. Police officers had to supervise our voting. You can see how in the midst of all of this, the land no longer seemed to be the issue. Yet, it was the issue all the time.

As I look back I refuse to give those opposing members the satisfaction of thinking that they were acting act out God's will by suing the church and causing havoc in the house of God. They were, in fact, doing God's will, but not like they thought. Their disturbance was simply the price I had to pay for my disobedience. As a result, I spent too many days in court. The church spent more than $150,000.00 in legal fees and the church was ultimately split. In my heart I believe to this day that the outcome would have been the same. That is, sooner or later, there would have been serious opposition or division over some other issue no matter what.

I truly believe that God has called me to create a ministry which was never meant for that traditional Baptist church. *Nevertheless, had I obeyed God, I might have fulfilled my calling without having to pay such a high cost.*

To show you just how good and gracious God is. After I left the church. I began a new church called Faith Ministries. Later, I went back to the owner of the original piece of land which we had voted on. That 30 acre site by the golf course. He told me that the land was still available and that he had decided that the only person he was going to sell it to was me. He said since I had decided not to buy it, he decided not to sell it.

I asked about the clause which required his permission to build anything else on the land. He said: "Oh that was just something that my lawyer threw in for my protection. You know how they are. We don't have to have that in there."

Then I said: "What about us having to approve of your selling alcohol." He said: "That was the lawyer too! I know I can't ask a church to approve the selling of alcohol. All I want you to do is to acknowledge that you know we do it as a part of our business and don't lead any campaigns to remove it."

Can you believe that? All we had to do was ask! We had assumed that God was not able to make a way in the beginning. Now, as I write, our new church, Faith Ministries, has purchased that 30 acre site by the golf course. By God's grace, we are going to build a city for Christian service and make disciples for Jesus Christ on the land very land we had asked God for in the first place. Believe me, I learned my lesson.

My sisters and my brothers take it from Saul and me, obedience to God is better than sacrifice and it surely is a lot cheaper too!

Triumph for Unconventional Pastors

Your First Church

Reverend Hosea was called to preach and then he was immediately assigned to a church. *The church of Gomer!* That is to say, the first place God sent the prophet Hosea to minister after he called him was to his own wife and family.

Granted, she was a prostitute. Granted her children were not simply born out of wedlock, but born in harlotry. Granted, she seemed to be incorrigible. Still, it was to his home that God sent Hosea first.

This was to accomplish several things:

1. ***It was to humble Hosea.*** Like any other preacher, the prophet Hosea probably would have enjoyed preaching to the multitudes. He would have loved proclaiming the word to the masses. But it seems that God was saying to him, before you preach to the whole world, maybe you should practice on your own house. If you can be faithful over a few things, I will make you ruler over many things.

2. ***It was to win Gomer.*** A second reason that God sent Hosea back home to minister might have been to save his own wife Gomer. This prophet like many of us have people in our own house who need to be saved. We have people in our own house who need to be healed. We have people in our own house who need ministry. We are not sent home, just for the practice. We are sent home because there is a need. Are there any Gomers in your house?

3. ***It was to model God's love.*** Lastly, to be mentioned here, God was making an example of Hosea. He was using the life of this prophet to show what His love for Israel was like. If you are a preacher and want to show something off, don't show me your degrees, don't show me your big church on the corner, don't show me your large sanctuary, don't show me your new car. Show me your wife and your children. If they love the Lord and are trying to follow Him, then I'll know how great a pastor you are.

When we turn the spotlight off of Hosea and shine it on us, we must admit that it is amazing how many preachers are sending out resumes and candidating for the big church down the street, when they are sorely neglecting the great church in their own house down the hall! I know because I did it for years.

After being a preacher all day, ministering to everybody you meet, praying at every public and private function, the last thing you want to do when you come home is minister. You want to kick off your shoes, watch the game, or just plain sleep.

What I did not realize was that my family was hurting in many ways just like me and in many instances because of me. I failed to see their ministry needs and therefore did not minister to them. I have written two books which speak to these matters. The first is called: *More Than 101 Ways to Turn Your Home into A Hallelujah House.* This book is for any family, not just the preacher's family. However, I do give concrete ways that a family can literally turn its home into an outpost of the kingdom.

The second book I have written along these lines is called the *ABC's of Effective Parenting*. In this work, I take each letter of the alphabet and offer a tip on parenting which begins with that letter. Here again, this book is for any one, but it does provide some simple ways to minister to your children within your own home.

I have been phenomenally blessed in my ministry. I have two degrees from Harvard. I have preached abroad. I have been given citations and awards by organizations and groups across the whole spectrum of society. I have preached at some of the most prestigious churches in America. Yet, of all the accomplishments that I have achieved, the greatest and most important to me is that I have a wife and four children who are all saved and serving the Lord. This, my friend, does not happen by osmosis. It happens by ministry.

Okay, I Admit It, I am a Dictator!

My secretary put a call through to my office one afternoon and on the other end was a reporter from the local daily newspaper. Being, as I was, in the midst of a great church upheaval and suspicious of the press, I was hesitant to even take the call. However, this young guy knew exactly what to say.

He introduced himself and began by buttering me up. He told me how much he had heard about me. How dynamic I was. How charismatic I was. How young I was. How energetic I was. How creative I was and in how much trouble I was! I don't know who or what his source was, but he had heard about the conflict in our church over building a new church and said that, personally, he thought I was getting a bum wrap. His newspaper wanted to do a feature story on me and get my side of the controversy out. He asked if he could come over and interview me.

Well, I don't believe it myself, but I actually bought his line and invited him over. When he arrived, he acted awestruck. He was so glad to meet me. I gave him a 25 cent tour of the church and as we walked I pumped him with my vision for the church in general and our church in particular. He followed me around with his little pad and wrote down everything I said. His photographer came a little later and took what seemed like a hundred shots to make sure he got a good one.

To be very honest, it was not that bad. He seemed friendly enough. I left the encounter feeling pretty good and thought that at last I would be able to get my point of view across through the muddled rumors and lies about me which were in the community air.

What the reporter did not tell me as he left was that his paper's policy was to get opposing views also. You know, for journalistic balance. Apparently, he went straight from his interview with me to interview some of the members of our church who were suing me! Wouldn't you know it, his feature article on me had to include them.

Knowing when the article was to be printed, but not knowing that I was not the only one going to be in it, I waiting anxiously for the day it was to hit my porch and, incidentally, the porches of 300,000 other homes in our metropolitan area! I knew from experience that good interviews do not always translate into good articles. Somehow, some very key and positive points invariably get lost in the sauce. Nevertheless, I thought this time would be different and I could not wait.

When day broke on that fateful Sunday morning, I *slowly* rushed down to the door to pick up the paper. Sure enough, on the front page of the metro section was a large picture of a stain glass window in our church and a multi-column article entitled: "Pastor, Members, clashing." Wait a minute. Was this the article about me? I guess so.

Still in my bathrobe and not altogether awake, I scanned the article trying to find something complimentary. In the dim light of my hallway, I actually did. He said of me, he is "Slight of stature, he comes across as larger than life, whether he is delivering his rhythmic Sunday sermons or meeting someone for the first time. He's smooth, a sweet talker, and has a boyish believability while appearing to be a mover and a shaker. He has the credentials to claim the latter title..."

That wasn't too bad, I thought, but when I got into the kitchen, turned on the bright light and began again to read the article, I saw a quote from one of the members in our church who was suing me. And this is what I've been leading up to all the time.

This one disgruntled member was quoted as saying: "I'm upset with the way he's doing things down there. He's a dictator." A dictator? *Moi?* Here, I was hoping to get a chance to communicate how fair and visionary I was and there it was right smack in the middle of the article. "He's a dictator."

In all fairness to the writer of the article, he did also quote another member who was all in favor of what we were trying to do. However, I must tell you that on that Sunday morning at the break of day all I could see on the page was "He's a dictator!"

I should not have been surprised. I had heard that people said that about me before. But no one had ever said it to my face and this was the first time that I (and 300,000 other people) had ever seen it in print!

In my heart and in his heart, both the man and I knew that I was not a dictator. Now, I know some pastors who missed their calling. They are more commandeering than George Patton! I know of pastors who hold business meetings and members must ask permission to leave even if they just have to go to the bathroom. If they are ever out of line they are told to sit down and shut up. There was none of that in me. Perhaps, that was my problem. I was too nice! Still, this member was getting at something significant when he called me a dictator, but what was it?

I think what this man was venting was not that I was mean or underhanded. It was just that in virtually every instance, I was clear on what I wanted. I knew what I did not want and I would not take one for the other. His was the frustration of a person who was seeing his church change radically before his eyes without any real power to stop it. I won most of the votes. I instituted most of the changes. I controlled the pulpit. I changed the order of worship. There was not much anyone could do about it.

What he didn't know was just how much I did listen to the people. He didn't know just how much my plans had been altered because of others. He didn't know just how much I did not have my way. He didn't know just how much more I would like to have changed. He didn't know just how soft my heart was when sincere opposition was raised. Nonetheless, from the way he kept score, I was changing everything and I did it by being a dictator.

I remember hearing people say that no one could talk to me. However, I also remember opening the door and inviting dialogue countless times, but very rarely would anyone respond.

After many years of this characterization being whispered about me, I have finally come to the place in my ministerial maturity where I gladly accept the designation. That's right. I admit it. I am a dictator, but not like that man thought.

It is an occupational hazard. As a man of God, it is my job to take dictation and to give dictation. When God speaks, I must sit still like John did on the isle of Patmos and just take down what the Lord has said.

Then, once I have received the word of the Lord, it is my duty to dictate it to those over whom the Lord has placed me. If I do not do it, then I am not true to my calling. What many church members resent and are frustrated by is that they cannot really get angry with the preacher who truly proclaims the truth without also getting upset with his, or her boss.

Now that I think of it, I am at my best when I am a dictator. That is, when I lose myself in the word of God, the will of God and the way of God and just dictate to the people "Thus saith the Lord." In fact, if the truth be told, I have gotten into the most trouble over these twenty some years of preaching when I failed to receive and deliver the Lord's dictation.

If you are an effective leader who gets things done no matter what, don't be surprised if you too aren't called a dictator. If you are a person in tune with God who preaches to a people who are out of tune with God, don't be surprised if you too are called a dictator. If you refuse to compromise the truth and won't back down from a fight for what's right, don't be surprised if you too aren't called a dictator.

I say to you something like what Jesus said to those who heard Him on the mount: *"When they call you a dictator for dictating the word of God, rejoice and be exceedingly glad, for great is your reward in heaven."*

Remember Who's Your Boss

One of the greatest and most fundamental lessons of ministry took me almost twenty years to learn. I had been preaching virtually all of my life and still didn't really know who I worked for. Let me tell you how I found out.

As you have already heard, our church was in the middle of a building program and we had engaged a stewardship company to come help us raise some significant dollars. In talking with our stewardship consultant, he mentioned that the program would only be successful if the leaders of the church made significant sacrificial gifts to the cause. When he said significant, he meant thousands of dollars.

Needless to say, since I was a preacher, my wife and I did not have thousands of dollars to give. So, we came up with a bright idea. My wife and I agreed that if we could not *give* thousands of dollars, maybe we could inspire our people by *giving up* thousands of dollars. That's exactly what we did.

I turned over my salary check each month for a year to the building fund and my family lived off of a love offering which was taken up for us each Sunday. Personally, I thought this was a great leap of faith. To commit to trust God and his people for a year should have inspired anyone to sacrifice. Right?

You will not believe what happened. The love offering was a disaster. First it was a disaster because most of the people in my church didn't mind me receiving a salary, but they were not going to give me money directly every week. Others did not participate because it looked like their pastor was begging. Still others didn't give because this was their opportunity to show their lack of love.

I admit that it was not done right. I should have taught the people about giving. I should have walked them through the scriptures which say that the servant is worthy of his hire and all of that, but I didn't. I assumed that they loved me and that would be enough. It wasn't. The bottom line was that there were only a few members who regularly and faithfully gave in those weekly offerings to support our family.

That was the worst year we ever had in terms of income directly from the church I served. But guess what? When we prepared our taxes the next year, we realized that during that year when the people of God did not respond as we thought that they would or should have, God did. We received more money that year from other sources than ever before. In all of our years of marriage, we had never earned as much money in one year as we did that year, but it did not come from the church people. It was sent from every other direction by God.

This taught me a lesson that I shall never forget. This lesson revolutionized my ministry from that point on. *I learned that just because a certain person signs your check, or votes on your annual raise does not mean that you work for them. As a preacher of the gospel you work for the Lord and He will take care of you regardless of what folk do, or don't do.*

After that experience, I just went crazy. I mean I didn't care if they were mad at me or not. I didn't worry if they opposed me, or not. I didn't fret if they didn't want to pay me or not. Suddenly, I was free. Whereas before, I agonized over what their possible reaction might be to anything I proposed, now I didn't have to worry about what they thought. *I may have been assigned to them, but I didn't work for them! I worked for God and He more than adequately paid me!*

Fear: The First and Final Frontier

At the end of the twenty-third psalm, David mentions two great twins who follow those that love the Lord. He says: "Surely goodness and mercy will follow me all the days of my life." What David does not tell us is that there is something else that stalks the faithful like a hungry lion after its prey. That is *fear*.

Wherever the people of God go, whatever they are called upon to do, however they are being used by God, they are always confronted with fear. No wonder over and over again in scripture, God had to tell His people: "Fear not!"

For the preacher attempting to speak the word to God's people and the pastor attempting to lead God's people, the first and last frontier he or she must overcome is fear.

Satan's most powerful two weapons are deception and fear. He deceives us and then, that with which he decieves us, frightens us!

This is why early on in the ministry of Jeremiah, one of the first things the Lord said to him when He called him was not to be afraid of the people's faces.

When a preacher or pastor is fearful, he or she is afraid to: present a visionary proposal; preach a prophetic sermon; make a creative suggestion; ask for an overdue raise; demand better treatment for himself/herself, or their family; try something unique and different; or challenge the status quo.

Fear is not all bad because there are some times when you and I should be afraid. We should be afraid if we disobey God like king Saul. We should be afraid if we forsake our calling like Jonah. We should be afraid if we lie like Ananias and Sapphira. We should be afraid if we betray the Lord like Judas. We should be afraid if we defy God like Pharaoh.

The fact of the matter is that we do face some rather fearsome situations. You've probably heard the story about that Black preacher who presented a bold new program to his church. At the conclusion of his oration he said: "If God be for us, who can be against us?" To this an old lady in the back shouted out: "These Negroes Reverend!"

These Negroes, nothwithstanding, in the faithful exercise of a God given task, you should fear not because of the negative side effects of fear.

Fear will keep you from:

1. ***Starting.*** You will be so afraid that you can never take the first step.

2. ***Standing.*** Once you have stepped out, fear will make you so nervous that you won't be able to stand.

3. ***Sticking.*** If you do manage to stand, fear will remove your "stickability." Your stand will never become a stride.

4. ***Stopping.*** Fear will brainwash you into believing that you could never quit a bad habit which you had no business beginning in the first place.

5. ***Stretching.*** You will never reach beyond your grasp because fear will ask you what's the use?

6. ***Striking.*** Time and time again you will miss golden opportunities to do great things for God because fear will not allow you to strike while the iron is hot.

Below you will find a list of what might be called ten of our greatest fears as preachers of the gospel:

1. ***Fear of folks' faces.*** We are afraid of how parishioners will look at us while we are talking and after we have spoken. We do not know what their faces mean. When they smile are they really happy or are the covering up a frown? When they frown are they really angry or are they just grouchy and don't know how to smile? Take my advice. If you can't find a friendly face. Don't look at the people at all. Preach to the clock on the wall in the back of the sanctuary!

2. ***Fear of lost fellowship.*** Virtually every preacher has periods of popularity. These times are so few and far between that the last thing you want to do is to jeopardize it by rocking the boat. Still, when God gives us a word, even though we know that it is from Him, we also know that once we deliver it, there will be those who depart from us. Jesus' experience of this is recorded in John 6. Nurture your fellowship with God. He will never leave you.

3. ***Fear of financial loss.*** This church is not just my calling. It is my job. It is my source of income. This is how I make my living. These are the people who feed my family. All of these and more may cross your mind before you take a bold and courageous stand for the

Lord. Keep in mind that your God is able to supply all of your needs according to His riches in glory.

4. ***Fear of living by faith.*** Paul said that we walk by faith and not by sight. Have you ever tried it. It can be rather scarry. This living by faith is not for the faint of heart. We know that we are called to follow God as Abraham did, but our trust in ourselves will not allow us to fully let go and let God. Faithful living can be extremely fruitful, but only after we overcome our fear of trying it.

5. ***Fear of failure.*** I am sure that I would have attempted far more for the Lord if I knew that I could not fail. The notion of failing has paralyzed me more than once. It wasn't so much failing as it was having people know that I had failed to meet my objectives. I can handle falling short in private, but it's the public embarrassment that I fear the most. Actually, this is one of the greatest traits of leadership. A leader is one who is willing to risk great failure in order to be a great success. You and I never fail as long as we are following God in obedience. For God, success by defintion is faithfulness.

6. ***Fear of your heavenly Father's disfavor.*** Have you ever compromised and didn't feel good about it. Have you ever be silent when you know you should have

opened your mouth? Have you ever closed your eyes to sin right in your midst? If you have and if you are a Christian, you know that it does not feel good to know that you are out of the will of God. In fact, you should be afraid when you realize it. The problem with this is that sometimes being in the will of God means that we must be out of the will and favor of men. When you must choose between the two, the will of man and the will of God, do like the apostles did. Say: "We must rather obey God than man."

7. ***Fear of family fall out.*** The decisions that we make in ministry not only effect our members, but they also effect our families. Moving from one city to another; accepting one parsonage over another; picking one issue to fight over another; and more can all have consquences for our familes. Since we love them, we do not want to intentionally hurt them. However, they are usually the first to feel the negative impact of what we say the Lord has called us to do.

8. ***Fear of success.*** I have already indicated that the fear of failure has paralyzed me more than once, but so has the fear of success. You would never think that some one could be afraid to succeed, but a person can. Once you succeed, then you are expected to do it again and again. What's worse is that you sense that people expect your next success to be greater than the last.

Success can be a lot of pressure which you may not want. Could this be why you keep getting to the brink of a break through and then falling back into the same old rut. You might be sabatoging yourself because you are afraid to succeed.

9. ***Fear of anonymity and insignificance.*** In the theme song to the television show *Cheers* the singer says he wants to go somewhere where everybody knows his name. This desire to be known by name is not only coveted by tavern patrons. It is also the secret plea of preachers. The greatest fear of many preachers is that they will serve a church for many years and in the twinkling of an eye, their presence and accomplishments will be forgotten. This might be why there are so many pictures of the pastor all over the church. This might be why the church has three choirs named after the pastor.

Worse than anonymity is the fear of *insignificance.* Anonymity is when no one knows who you are or what you did. Insiginificance is when everyone may know who you are, but what you did was of absolutely no value! My motto is: "If I'm going to be crucified, you had better believe it's going to be for something of significance."

10. Fear of death. This fear is by no means placed last because it is the least. As a matter of fact, all of those which preceed it are some form of it. The fear of death does not only refer to physical death, but the absence of aspects of our lives which we cherish. Paul said that he died daily. So do we. However, it is not until we overcome the fear of death that we actually begin to live. This is the reason why Jesus had to die. By dying and rising from the dead, He overcame our most fundamental foe. In so doing, He has also given us reason not to fear death.

Now that we know some of the side effects of fear and have a list of ten of our greatest fears, how, then, can we overcome our fears?

1. Associate with fearless people. You will develop your boldness as you watch and tag along with fearless people. In the process, you will also find that these models also have their own fears, but they do not keep them from acting on faith.

2. Build on past successes. Even the most fearful among us have some successes in our past. We must learn how to remember and build upon these.

3. Nike philosphy. There's no other way to say it but: "Take a big gulp and Just Do It!"

4. ***Shift the weight on Him.*** When we shift the weight on the Lord. It becomes His responsibility to bring us through. Why then should we fear? They that *weight* upon the Lord shall renew their strength!"

5. ***Take baby steps until you are confident in making great strides.*** Chop your task up into small pieces and then the whole job may not appear so fearsome.

Could it be that you are where you are in ministry because you are afraid to be where you belong. All along you have blamed your education, your poverty, your opportunity and your small church. However, it just might be *your fear* that has been holding you back.

In the name of God and under the anointing of Christ I bid you go forth and do what you must do, be what you've been called to be, build what you have been commissioned to build, preach what you must preach and while you're doing it - *fear not!*

"Start Shaking!"

My brothers and sisters in the ministry, the clock is ticking. The day is fading. The sun is setting. Your life is passing. And you have a decision to make.

Are you going to continue to be strapped and trapped in an environment which crushes your creativity and saps the joy juice out of your soul? Are you going to maintain business as usual and just pray that things will get better all by themselves? Are you going to keep on having your God given proposals handed out and then put out with the next day's trash? Are you going to keep listening to what man says and not do what God says?

Or, are you going to take a step towards your personal freedom and God's heavenly kingdom? Are you going to remain trapped, or have you made up your mind, come hell or high water, I must be and shall be free to serve the Lord?

It seems to me that in order to be free, you have at least four options and all of them involve *shaking*.

Shake in Your Boots and Be Rejected

Remember King Saul? Don't ever forget him. He was a handsome, favored, anointed and chosen man. Nevertheless, he was rejected by God and put off of Israel's throne simply because of his disobedience. What in the world would make a king jeopardize so much?

These are the words he used to explain his sin to the prophet Samuel: *"I have sinned; for I have transgressed the commandment of the Lord, and thy words;* ***because I feared the people, and obeyed their voice****." (I Samuel 15:24)*

In other words, his fear of the people over whom God had given him authority, made him *shake in his boots*. This fear is what made him reluctant to do what he knew was God's will for his personal life and God's plan for Israel's national life.

If you like, you can allow the fear of your people to keep you from following through on God's call and commandments to you. However, if you do, you will risk being rejected and replaced by God just as Saul was.

Shake Down the House and Die

This is what Samson did. The story is found in Judges 16:21-31. You will recall that Delilah had betrayed him into the hands of the Philistines who in turn put him into prison. After many days, the Philistines were having a feast and they wanted to be amused, so they called for Samson to entertain them with a display of his strength.

By that time, Samson was blind and had to be led around by the hand. During the feast, he asked to be shown where the supporting pillars of the room were. Then, he walked over to them and pushed them down until the whole building fell in. The collapse of the building killed several thousand Philistines *and* Samson as well.

While this is clearly not an option which I recommend, it is one which many preachers and pastors are pursuing. They are allowing vengeance, pride and spite to make them fight and fight and fight to the bitter end, even if it destroys the church and kills them. Be careful how you shake down the Lord's house, it may fall in on you!

Shake up the House and Stay

When you get a chance, do yourself a favor. *Read* and *study* chapters 22-24 of II Kings. There you will find the interesting and inspiring story of Josiah. This young man was the son of a wicked king named Amon. Yet, at the age of eight he ascended to the throne of Israel and did what was right in the sight of the Lord.

Josiah's great claim to fame is the religious reforms he instituted in the eighteenth year of his reign. During that time, a book of God's law was found in the temple as workers were renovating it. The young king had the law read to him. He wept and rent his clothes when he realized how far Israel had strayed away from God's commandments.

Josiah refused to allow Israel to continue in sin. Therefore, he proceeded to tear down the altars of idol gods; kill all the false prophets; outlaw immoral practices; ban child sacrifice and call Israel to a new level of holiness. *Josiah was not afraid of the people. He was more afraid of God.* Thus, he stayed there and *shook up the house* until it was in the shape that God wanted it to be.

I don't have the time or space to unpack Josiah's story in detail, but before you go off copying his example, notice the following three factors which he had in his favor.

1. His people had and demonstrated a sense of justice and faith. They knew right from wrong and they did what was right. We see this in II Kings 21:23-26. There, after the assassination of his father Amon, the people made Josiah king even though he was only eight years old and even though his daddy had been a crook.

2. Josiah did not begin his major reforms in Israel until his eighteenth year as king. True enough, at that time he was still young, only 26 years of age. However, *he had been on the throne for eighteen years before he shook the house*. (II Kings 22:3)

3. Josiah read the words of the law to the people. When they heard it, they "stood to it" and covenanted with Josiah to keep every word of the law. Thus, he was able to make such drastic changes because he was blessed with a people who were *teachable* and *willing* to do the word of God, once they knew and understood it. (II Kings 23:3)

If your church is bound in traditions and is structured out of line with God's word, you can help them get into line. It will *not* be easy, but you won't mind it as much if your people are teachable and willing; and if *you* are persistent and patient.

Shake off the Dust and Leave

This is what Jesus (*and I*) did. When He went home to Nazareth (Mark 6:1-6), He found out that He could do no great miracles there. The hearts of the people were too hard. The faith of the people was too weak. The reception of His own home town was too cold.

Did Jesus sit at the gates of the city and cry? No! Did He go back to His kinsmen and beg them to believe? No! Did He remain in that familiar town and suffer rejection, ridicule and abuse? No! He simply "went round about the villages, teaching."

It is right after this in Mark 6:7-12 where Jesus sends forth his disciples to *other* towns to preach. He says to them in effect: "Take nothing for your journey. Go where you are received and do not remain where you are not received. In fact, when you leave a city which rejects you and the gospel which you preach, shake the very dust of that city off of your feet. Then, keep on stepping to other towns and cities which will receive you gladly."

In my case, I knew that God had conceived a great ministry in me. For years, I tried and tried to bring it forth in a traditional church environment. Like a pregnant woman, I felt the baby kicking inside of me, I saw signs of its life all around, and I even had labor pains pressing me. Nevertheless, it would not come forth.

Many were the days that I wanted to abort it or have someone else would adopt it. But, it was not to be. This was *my* baby and *I* had to bear it. When it was finally clear to me that my traditional church neither understood it, nor wanted it, God released me to more freely follow after Him.

I shook the dust from off of my feet in November of 1991. The baby was, indeed, born. Her name is *Faith Ministries*. Thanks be to God, she is doing just fine!

You don't have to do what I have done. In fact, *if the Lord is not leading you to do so, you better not even think about it*. Still, I am where I am in ministry today because I finally came to the conclusion that I could not wait for my church to set me free. I had to boldly seize my freedom, whether they liked it or not. I didn't have to be rude. I didn't have to be mean. I didn't have to be hard to get along with. But, I did have to be determined, if I wanted to be free.

My brothers and sisters, as a preacher who has been liberated from a traditional church, let me confess to you that everything is not peaches and cream now! However, I will assure you that freedom is far better than bondage!

Whatever you choose to do is between you and God. However, you must choose. You cannot go on living beneath your calling as you are. *That is no place for a prophet.*

By the grace of God you can be free! Go ahead step out on faith. As long as you follow *Him*, God will never fail you.

A Concluding Sermonic Post Script

"No Place for a Prophet"
I Kings 19:9-13

No Place for a Prophet

Some things just don't belong in certain places. An oven is no place for a snowball. A pig pen is no place for a pearl. A tree is no place for a trout. An ocean is no place for an ostrich. A river bed is no place for a robin. And a cave is no place for a prophet!

Caves are for blind bats. Caves are for hibernating bears. Caves are for slimy bugs. Caves are for wildly beasts. This is no place for a prophet!

You expect to see a prophet in conference with God. You expect to see a prophet in confrontation with unrighteousness. You expect to see a prophet in conversation with his colleagues. You expect to see a prophet in communication with kings. However, the last place you would ever look for, or expect to find a prophet is in a cave. This is no place for a prophet!

A cave is a dark place, but the prophet is supposed to represent the light. A cave is a dismal place, but the prophet is supposed to be the bearer of joy. A cave is a cold place, but the prophet should bring down fire from on high. This is no place for a prophet!

What Doeth Thou Here?

Nevertheless, despite the fact that this is no place for a prophet, it is exactly where we find the prophet Elijah - in a cave. He is sentimental. He is suicidal. He is weary. He is weeping. He is wounded.

When Adam went into hiding after he and Eve had sinned, God asked him: “Where art thou?” But, when Elijah went into hiding, God just wanted to know what he was doing there. The Lord asked this prophet: “What doeth thou here, Elijah?”

The prophet replied: “I have been very jealous for the Lord God of hosts: for the children of Israel have forsaken thy covenant, thrown down thine altars, and slain thy prophets with the sword: and I, even I only am left; and they seek my life, to take it away.”

Still, I do not believe that all of the prophet’s response has not been recorded. Would you allow me, therefore, to use my sanctified imagination and suggest several reasons which are implied by, but never printed in, the text?

Elijah was there in that cave because he was running from responsibility. He was in that cave because Queen Jezebel was after him. Elijah had confronted her prophets of Baal on Mt. Carmel. Not only did Elijah and his God outshine those prophets of Baal, Elijah went so far as to kill them. All 450 of them! This enraged Jezebel and she vowed to kill him. Thus, Elijah was willing to take the responsibility of standing up for God on Mt. Carmel, but he was not willing to be responsible for the fall out of such a courageous stand.

Elijah was in that cave rationalizing his reaction. In effect, he said the reason that I am in this cave is because the rest of Israel has forsaken the Lord's covenant; thrown down His altars and slain His prophets. Elijah rationalized that he had every right to be in that cave because he was the only true believer left and *his* very life was in jeopardy. Both he and God had become an endangered species. If he did not save himself, the cause of God would be decisively damaged.

Then, while Elijah was in that cave, he was restricting his reach. Here was a man called to preach to the whole world and now his ministry had been reduced to a cave. He had a message for the masses and here he was in a cave. Who could be converted in a cave? To whom could he preach in a cave? Who could hear the gospel in a cave? He was restricting his reach through a self- inflicted isolation and withdrawal from the world.

What Drives A Prophet Here

This was no place for a prophet, but there was almost no way he could have avoided ending up here after what he did. What did he do? What is it that drove this prophet to this point?

The first thing is that he dared to deliver the word of God. At the command of God, he went to king Ahab and declared that there would be no rain until he said so. There would be no rain because of the king's unrighteousness. Notice that after he preached there would be no rain, not only did the rain stop, but the brook dried up too. In fact, *Elijah's* brook dried up. The place where the prophet had found refreshment in the draught also dried up. In other words, he too was effected by the word he preached.

By daring to deliver the word of God, he found himself being accused of troubling Israel. The word of God is always troubling if you are caught on the wrong side of it. It has been known to comfort the afflicted and afflict the comfortable.

Then, secondly, Elijah was driven to such a place because he had the courage to challenge false prophets. Elijah would have been all right if he had just overlooked the issue of idolatry in Israel and walked away. However, he got into trouble because he challenged the prophets of Baal directly, personally and publicly.

Like Joshua he said: "How long halt ye between two opinions. If the Lord be God, follow him: but if Baal, then follow him." No matter how polished, professional, prolific and persuasive the false prophets may be, the issue is not friendship, or family relationship. It's all about His Lordship and our discipleship. There will be no rain until the matter of who the real God is has been resolved.

A third factor that drove Elijah to this point was what might be called "the agony of victory." You may remember that ABC's Wide World of Sports telecast used to open with a scene of a victorious athlete with the words "The thrill of victory..." heard behind him. Then, it would show a poor soul sliding down and off of a ski slope with the words "The agony of defeat" being heard behind him. What we have here is somewhat different.

This is neither the thrill of victory, nor the agony of defeat. Elijah is suffering from the *agony of victory*. The agony of victory is when you are a winner, but you feel like a loser. It is when you have reached for fulfillment and found only emptiness.

Believe it, or not, sometimes it is easier to lose than to win. When you lose, no one expects much of you. But when you win, they expect the world from you.

Why is it that being right and winning a battle does not always make you happy? You can become a victim of victory. Winners become easy and automatic targets of attacks. People want your visibility, but not your responsibility.

You see, since Jezebel didn't know God and could not get back at God, she did the next best thing which was attack God's representative. Elijah didn't send down the fire. God did. Yet, His messenger was the one who received the wrath of the wicked.

Another angle on the agony of victory is the fact that Elijah's success was a *solo success*. Some people cannot imagine why Elijah should be sad after all he had done. He stopped the rain. He kept a widow's meal barrel full. He raised a dead lad. He slew 450 prophets of Baal. He started the rain falling again. He should have been the happiest person in town. But he was not.

He was extremely successful, however, he had a solo success. He had no one to share the fight. He had no one to share the victory. He had no one to share the agony. Perhaps, people would say that he deserved to be alone because after all, he tried to do it all by himself. But he had to fight alone, no one else would stand with him.

Remember, I Kings 18:21, “the people answered not a word.” It seems as if the people who boo you and criticize you, use a microphone, while those who support you, do so in silent prayer.

The Prophet as Quarterback

I know how Elijah must have felt. Sometimes, I feel like a quarterback. He handles the ball on every play. Always in the spotlight. His name is in the paper. He is the talk of the town. He has an excellent record with far more wins than losses.

I must admit that in the past twenty years, I have enjoyed being a quarterback. In fact, I am guilty at times of trying to play all of the positions not only because I liked it, but because I did not have full confidence in the rest of my team.

But after a while, despite the glory and attention, even quarterbacks get tired. The problem is that even though they may win every game, the quarterback gets hit on every play. *He gets hit because the other team knows that he has the ball and he is the center of the offense. Then, he gets hit because his own team mates telegraph his plays to the opposition and they blitz him on his weak side. Even if the team scores a touch down, the quarterback still gets hit.* After a while, you just get tired of being hit and tackled.

The Lord blessed our ministry and every time I thought I scored a touch down, I got hit.

- I sought to preach the gospel outdoors in a nearby housing development and it was said that I was degrading the gospel. Touch down, but I got hit.

- I literally turned somersaults in a One Man Show which I sponsored to reach and save young souls. I was called undignified. Touch down, but I got hit.

- I translated the gospel in to rap for today's young people, became "The Rappin Reverend" and it was said that I was using the devil's music. Touch down, but I got hit.

- I visited 50 area schools and got 18,000 youths to commit to live drug free, alcohol free and crime free lives and I was told that I should have been visiting the sick and shut-in instead. Touch down, but I got hit.

- I reached out through in a radio ministry to 80 of the 88 counties in the state of Ohio and was told that it cost too much money. Touch down, but I got hit.

- I created a series called the *ABC's of Effective Parenting* which aired regularly on the a secular radio station and I was told that because I was a preacher, it had no business on a rhythm and blues station. Touch down, but I got hit.

- We formed a community development corporation, purchased an $18 million housing development for only $3.00 and simply because they didn't understand how tax credits worked, people said that it must have been crooked. Touch down, but I got hit.

- I turned in my salary for a year, lived on faith off of a love offering and was called a con artist. Touch down, but I got hit.

I know what it's like to be a success and yet want to run into a cave simply because you are tired of being hit!

What's A Prophet To Do?

So, what then is this prophet to do? Ahab is after him. Jezebel has vowed to kill him. God is calling him. Here's what God told Elijah to do.

1. ***"Go!"*** (v.15) Get out of this cave. Your were not meant for it. You were not called for it. I will not have it. Get out of this cave. Close down your pity party. Dry up your tears. Snap out of your depression. Stop your complaining. Get back to work. Get out of this cave!

2. ***Recruit and anoint new leadership.*** (vvs.15-17) When you get out of the cave, the first thing I want you to do is to seek out and anoint some new leadership. Anoint Hazael to be king over Syria. Anoint Jehu to be king over Israel in Ahab's place. Anoint Elisha to be a prophet in your place. The new work which I am about to do will require a new and anointed leadership. And besides, you no longer need to carry this load alone. I am promoting you from quarterback to coach! They will be ministers to you and they will clean the house of God for me!

3. ***Minister to the 7000 you have overlooked.*** (v. 18) You have been so busy running from Jezebel and fighting with false prophets that you have overlooked

a host of faithful people right in your midst. You are not the only one who loves the Lord. You are not the only one who serves Him sincerely. You are not the only one who desires righteousness. You are not the only prophet I have left. You are not alone. I have 7000 people in Israel who are faithful to me and have never bowed their knees to Baal.

Take your mind off of Ahab and Jezebel. Let me take care of them. Stop worrying about false prophets. I'll shut their mouths. All I want you to do is go back through the wilderness and call out the others who are also in hiding. Preach to them. Minister to them. Witness to them. Prophesy to them. Disciple them. Teach them. Anoint them. Lead them. Worship me with them. And when you do, then will I abundantly bless you!